THE ULTIMATE GUIDE TO EARNING MONEY ON THE INTERNET:

Introduction:

In today's digital age, the internet offers a multitude of opportunities to earn money from the comfort of your own home. Whether you're looking to supplement your income, start a new career, or pursue a passion project, making money online has become increasingly accessible. From freelance work and online surveys to e-commerce and digital marketing, the online space provides a diverse range of avenues for generating income. With the right skills, dedication, and entrepreneurial spirit, individuals can leverage the power of the internet to create sustainable and profitable sources of revenue.

Making money is a goal that many people strive for, and there are countless ways to achieve it. Whether you're looking to supplement your income, save for a big purchase, or even start a new career, there are numerous opportunities available to help you reach your financial goals. From traditional employment to entrepreneurial ventures, the key to making money lies in identifying your skills, interests, and resources, and leveraging them to create value for others.

One of the most common ways to make money is through traditional employment. This can involve working for a company or organization in exchange for a regular pay-check. Whether you're in an entry-level position or a high-level executive role, traditional employment offers a steady and reliable source of income. However, it may also come with limitations in terms of earning potential and flexibility. Many people find that they are able to increase their income by seeking out new job opportunities, pursuing additional education or training, or taking on side gigs and freelance work.

Another avenue for making money is through entrepreneurial endeavours. This can involve starting your own business, whether it's a small-scale venture operated from home or a larger enterprise with multiple employees. Entrepreneurship offers the potential for unlimited earning potential and the ability to be your own boss. However, it also comes with significant risks and challenges, including the need for start-up capital, the responsibility of managing all aspects of the business, and the potential for failure. Nonetheless, many people find that the rewards of entrepreneurship - including financial independence, creative freedom, and the opportunity to make a meaningful impact - make it a worthwhile pursuit.

In addition to traditional employment and entrepreneurship, there are numerous other ways to make money. This can include investing in stocks, real estate, or other assets; providing services as a freelancer or consultant; creating and selling products online; participating in the gig economy through platforms like Uber or TaskRabbit; or even earning passive income through royalties, licensing agreements, or affiliate marketing. Each of these opportunities comes with its own set of advantages and challenges, and the key is to find the right fit for your skills, interests, and goals.

Regardless of the specific path you choose to pursue, there are several key principles that can help you succeed in making money. First and foremost, it's important to identify your strengths and interests, as well as any gaps in the market that you can fill. By leveraging your unique skills and experiences, you can create value for others and differentiate yourself from the competition. Additionally, it's important to stay informed about current trends and developments in your industry, as well as to continuously seek out new opportunities for growth and improvement.

Furthermore, it's essential to be disciplined and proactive in managing your finances. This includes creating a budget, setting financial goals, and regularly tracking your income and expenses. By being mindful of your spending habits and making strategic decisions about how to allocate your resources, you can maximize your earning potential and build long-term financial stability.

In conclusion, making money is a multifaceted endeavour that requires creativity, resourcefulness, and perseverance. Whether you choose to pursue traditional employment, start your own business, or explore other avenues for generating income, the key is to identify opportunities that align with your skills and interests, and to approach them with dedication and strategic thinking. By staying informed, being disciplined in your financial management, and continually seeking out new opportunities for growth and improvement, you can position yourself for success in achieving your financial goals.

Chapter 1
Take Online Surveys:

Online surveys are a method of gathering information and feedback from a targeted audience through the internet. These surveys are typically conducted using survey software or online platforms, allowing participants to respond to a series of questions and prompts. Online surveys can cover a wide range of topics, including market research, customer satisfaction, employee feedback, and social research.

One of the key advantages of online surveys is their accessibility and convenience. Participants can easily access and complete surveys from any location with an internet connection, eliminating the need for face-to-face interactions or paper-based questionnaires. This accessibility also allows for a larger and more diverse pool of respondents, potentially providing more representative and insightful data.

Online surveys also offer flexibility in terms of survey design and administration. Researchers can easily customize the format and structure of the survey to suit their specific needs, incorporating various question types such as multiple choice, open-ended responses, rating scales, and more. Additionally, the automated nature of online surveys streamlines the data collection and analysis process, saving time and resources for researchers.

Furthermore, online surveys can provide a level of anonymity for participants, which may encourage more honest and candid responses. This can be particularly valuable when addressing sensitive or personal topics. The ability to track responses and analyze data in real-time also allows for quick insights and decision-making based on the survey results.

However, there are also potential limitations to consider when using online surveys. Issues such as response bias, sample representativeness, and survey fatigue can impact the reliability and validity of the data collected. Researchers must carefully consider these factors when designing and interpreting online surveys.

Overall, online surveys offer a convenient and efficient means of gathering valuable information and feedback from a wide audience. When used thoughtfully and in conjunction with other research methods, online surveys can provide valuable insights for businesses, organizations, and researchers alike.

There are so many steps to follow while doing online surveys.
Research Survey Sites: Look for reputable survey websites that offer cash rewards for completing surveys. Ensure that the sites have positive reviews and a history of paying their users.
Online surveys are a popular method of data collection used by businesses, researchers, and organizations to gather information from a targeted audience. These surveys are conducted over the internet and can be accessed and completed by respondents at their convenience. Online surveys offer a cost-effective and efficient way to gather large amounts of data, and they can be tailored to specific demographics or target groups.

One of the key advantages of online surveys is their accessibility. With the widespread use of the internet and digital devices, surveys can reach a large and diverse audience, including people from different geographical locations. This accessibility also allows for a quicker response time, as respondents can complete the survey at a time that suits them, reducing the need for scheduling and coordination.

Online surveys also offer flexibility in terms of survey design and question types. Researchers can use a variety of question formats, such as multiple-choice, open-ended, Likert scales, and more, to gather different types of data. This flexibility allows for a more comprehensive understanding of the respondents' opinions, attitudes, and behaviours.

Furthermore, online surveys can be designed to be interactive and engaging, which can help increase response rates and reduce survey fatigue. Features such as progress bars, skip logic, and multimedia elements can make the survey experience more enjoyable for respondents, leading to more accurate and thoughtful responses.

In addition to being cost-effective and efficient, online surveys also offer quick data analysis and reporting. Once the survey is completed, the data can be automatically compiled and analyzed, providing researchers with immediate insights. This real-time data collection and analysis can be invaluable for businesses and organizations looking to make timely decisions based on current trends and feedback.

However, there are also some limitations to consider when using online surveys. One of the main challenges is ensuring the representativeness of the sample. As not everyone has access to the internet or may be willing to participate in online surveys, there is a risk of selection bias. Researchers need to carefully consider ways to mitigate this bias, such as using stratified sampling or combining online surveys with other data collection methods.

Another potential limitation is the issue of survey fraud or dishonest responses. Without face-to-face interaction, it can be more challenging to verify the authenticity of respondents and ensure that they are providing truthful answers. Researchers can implement measures such as captcha verification, attention checks, and data validation to minimize fraudulent responses.

In conclusion, online surveys are a valuable tool for gathering data from a wide range of respondents in a cost-effective and efficient manner. Their accessibility, flexibility, and quick data analysis make them an attractive option for businesses and researchers looking to gather insights from their target audience. However, it is important to be mindful of the potential limitations and take steps to address them in order to ensure the validity and reliability of the survey results.

To research a good online survey, you can follow these steps:

Define Your Objectives: Clearly outline the purpose of your survey and the specific information you want to gather.

Choose a Survey Tool: Look for reputable online survey tools that offer a range of features, such as customizable survey templates, data analysis tools, and result reporting.

Review User Reviews and Ratings: Check online reviews and ratings for different survey tools to gauge user satisfaction and the tool's effectiveness.

Compare Features: Compare the features offered by different survey tools, such as question types, survey distribution options, and data analysis capabilities.

Consider Pricing: Evaluate the pricing plans of various survey tools to ensure they fit within your budget and offer value for money.

Test the Tool: If possible, take advantage of free trials or demo versions to test the usability and functionality of the survey tools before making a final decision.

Check Customer Support: Look for survey tools that provide reliable customer support in case you encounter any issues or need assistance.

Ensure Data Security: Verify that the survey tool has robust data security measures in place to protect the confidentiality of survey responses and personal information.

Sign Up: Create accounts on multiple survey sites to increase your earning potential. Provide accurate information about yourself during the registration process.
To sign up for online surveys, you can follow these general steps:

Choose a Survey Platform: Select a reputable online survey platform that offers opportunities to participate in surveys and earn rewards.

Create an Account: Visit the website of the survey platform and look for a "Sign Up" or "Create Account" option. Provide the required information to create your account, such as your name, email address, and a password.

Complete Your Profile: After creating your account, complete your profile by providing additional details such as your demographic information, interests, and preferences. This information helps the survey platform match you with relevant survey opportunities.

Verify Your Email: Some survey platforms may require you to verify your email address by clicking on a verification link sent to your email inbox.

Explore Available Surveys: Once your account is set up, log in to the survey platform and explore the available surveys. You may be able to filter surveys based on different criteria such as length, reward type, and topic.

Participate in Surveys: Select surveys that interest you and participate by providing honest and thoughtful responses to the survey questions.

Earn Rewards: Depending on the survey platform, you may earn rewards such as cash, gift cards, or other incentives for completing surveys.

It's important to note that different survey platforms may have varying signup processes and requirements, so it's best to follow the specific instructions provided by the platform you choose to sign up with.

Ways Completing Profile Surveys: Many survey sites require you to fill out profile surveys to match you with relevant survey opportunities. Completing these surveys can lead to more targeted opportunities. Completing good surveys can lead to more targeted opportunities in several ways:

Enhanced Profile Matching: By providing accurate and detailed information in your survey responses, you help survey platforms build a more comprehensive profile of your interests, preferences, and demographics. This allows them to match you with surveys that are more relevant to your profile, resulting in a better fit for your interests and experiences.

Quality Responses: Providing thoughtful and high-quality responses to survey questions demonstrates your engagement and reliability as a survey participant. Survey platforms may take note of participants who consistently provide valuable feedback, leading to more targeted opportunities being presented to them.

Increased Trust and Reputation: Consistently completing surveys with integrity and attention to detail can enhance your reputation as a reliable survey participant. This can lead to survey platforms offering you more targeted opportunities, as they trust that you will provide valuable insights.

Access to Specialized Surveys: Some surveys are designed for specific demographics or niche interests. By consistently participating in surveys and demonstrating expertise in certain areas, you may gain access to specialized surveys that are tailored to your expertise and experiences.

Exclusive Opportunities: Survey platforms may offer exclusive or high-paying survey opportunities to participants who have demonstrated dedication and quality participation in the past. These exclusive opportunities are often more targeted and may offer higher rewards.

In summary, completing good surveys with accuracy, thoughtfulness, and consistency can lead to survey platforms recognizing your value as a participant and offering you more targeted opportunities that align with your interests and expertise.

Cash Out Your Earnings: Once you accumulate a certain amount of earnings, cash out your rewards according to the payment options provided by the survey sites. Some sites offer PayPal payments, gift cards, or direct deposits. It's important to review the cash-out options provided by the specific survey platform you are using, as the availability of different redemption methods may vary. Additionally, consider factors such as minimum redemption thresholds, processing times, and any associated fees when choosing your preferred cash-out method.

There are several common ways to cash out or redeem rewards from your online survey account. Here are some of the most popular methods:

1. PayPal: Many survey platforms offer PayPal as a cash-out option, allowing you to transfer your survey earnings directly to your PayPal account.

2. Gift Cards: Survey platforms often provide the option to redeem your earnings in the form of gift cards from popular retailers, online stores, or service providers.

3. Bank Transfer: Some survey platforms allow you to transfer your survey earnings directly to your bank account through a secure electronic transfer.

4. Prepaid Debit Cards: Certain survey platforms offer prepaid debit cards as a cash-out option, which can be used for purchases or cash withdrawals.

5. Charitable Donations: Some survey platforms allow you to donate your earnings to charitable organizations or causes of your choice.

6. Merchandise and Products: In addition to cash rewards, some survey platforms offer the option to redeem earnings for merchandise, products, or services.

Stay Progressive and Consistent: To maximize your earnings, consistently check for new survey opportunities and complete surveys whenever they are available. Consistency is quite important as to give ways for progressiveness in financial income. The more online survey you do, the more money you make as time progresses.

Protect Your Privacy: Be cautious about sharing personal information and avoid survey sites that request sensitive data such as Social Security numbers or financial information.
Protecting your personal information online is essential for maintaining your privacy and security. Here are several ways to safeguard your personal information when using the internet:

a. Use Strong, Unique Passwords: Create strong and unique passwords for your online accounts, and avoid using the same password across multiple websites. Consider using a reputable password manager to securely store and manage your passwords. Example of strong password; R.Mdta&75@idnL.13d

b. Enable Two-Factor Authentication (2FA): Whenever possible, enable two-factor authentication for your online accounts. 2FA adds an extra layer of security by requiring a secondary verification method, such as a code sent to your mobile device.

c. Be Cautious with Personal Information: Avoid sharing sensitive personal information, such as your full name, address, phone number, and social security number, on public websites and social media platforms.

d. Use Secure Wi-Fi Networks: When accessing the internet, use secure and trusted Wi-Fi networks to reduce the risk of unauthorized access to your data.

e. Update Privacy Settings: Regularly review and update the privacy settings on your social media accounts, email accounts, and other online platforms to control who can see your personal information.

f. Be Wary of Phishing Attempts: Be cautious of unsolicited emails, messages, or calls that request personal information or prompt you to click on suspicious links. Phishing attempts often aim to steal personal information.

g. Secure Your Devices: Keep your devices (such as computers, smartphones, and tablets) updated with the latest security patches and use reputable antivirus and anti-malware software to protect against threats.

h.   Use Secure Websites: When providing personal information or making online transactions, ensure that the websites are secure by looking for "https://" in the URL and a padlock icon in the address bar.

i.   Review Privacy Policies: Review the privacy policies of websites and online services to understand how your personal information is collected, used, and shared.

j.   Educate Yourself: Stay informed about common online privacy risks and best practices for protecting your personal information. Regularly review resources from reputable sources on online privacy and security.

Why protecting privacy is very significant:

Protecting privacy is very significant when doing online surveys for several reasons. First and foremost, individuals have a right to privacy, and it is important to respect and uphold this right in all aspects of data collection, including online surveys. When individuals participate in online surveys, they are often providing personal information about themselves, their preferences, and their behaviours. This information can be sensitive and private, and it is essential to safeguard it from unauthorized access or misuse.

Furthermore, protecting privacy in online surveys helps to build trust between the survey administrators and the participants. When individuals feel that their privacy is being respected and protected, they are more likely to provide honest and accurate responses. This is crucial for the validity and reliability of the survey data. If participants are concerned that their privacy may be compromised, they may be reluctant to fully engage with the survey or may provide inaccurate information, leading to biased or unreliable results.

In addition, ensuring privacy in online surveys is important for compliance with data protection regulations and ethical standards. Many jurisdictions have laws and regulations that govern the collection, storage, and use of personal data, and survey administrators have a responsibility to adhere to these requirements. Failure to protect the privacy of survey participants can result in legal consequences and damage to the reputation of the organization conducting the survey.

Moreover, maintaining privacy in online surveys helps to mitigate the risk of data breaches and unauthorized access to sensitive information. With the increasing prevalence of cyber threats and hacking incidents, it is essential for survey administrators to implement robust security measures to safeguard the personal data collected through online surveys. This includes using secure data storage systems, encryption techniques, and access controls to prevent unauthorized disclosure or misuse of the information.

Overall, protecting privacy in online surveys is crucial for respecting individuals' rights, building trust with participants, complying with regulations, and mitigating security risks. By prioritizing privacy protection in the design and implementation of online surveys, organizations can ensure the integrity and credibility of the data collected while demonstrating their commitment to ethical and responsible data practices.

By implementing these measures, you can take proactive steps to protect your personal information and minimize the risk of unauthorized access or misuse of your data online.

Manage Expectations:

Online surveys may not provide substantial income, but they can be a way to earn extra cash in your free time. Devote time on your free times and do as many online surveys as you can.

Types of expectations to manage when doing online surveys:

When conducting online surveys, it's important to manage various types of expectations to ensure the success of the research. Firstly, it's crucial to set realistic expectations for the response rate. While online surveys can reach a wide audience, not everyone will respond, so it's important to anticipate and account for a lower response rate than traditional methods. Additionally, managing expectations around the level of detail in responses is important. Participants may provide brief or limited answers, so researchers should be prepared for varying levels of depth in the data collected.

Furthermore, it's important to consider and manage expectations around the timing of the survey process. This includes setting realistic timelines for data collection, analysis, and reporting. Managing expectations around the scope of the survey is also critical. Clearly defining the objectives and limitations of the survey can help prevent unrealistic expectations about the insights that can be gained.

Another important aspect is managing expectations around data quality. Online surveys may be susceptible to response bias or inaccuracies, so researchers should be transparent about the potential limitations and take steps to minimize these issues. Additionally, it's important to manage expectations around confidentiality and privacy. Participants should be assured that their responses will be kept confidential and used only for research purposes.

Lastly, managing expectations around the impact of the survey is essential. Researchers should communicate realistic expectations about how the survey results will be used and the potential impact of the research findings. By proactively addressing these various types of expectations, researchers can ensure that their online surveys are conducted effectively and yield valuable insights.

By following these steps above, you can start making money by taking online surveys for cash.

Chapter 2
Freelancing and remote work Opportunities.

Freelancing and remote work opportunities refer to the ability for individuals to work independently and outside of a traditional office setting. Freelancing typically involves working on a project or contract basis for multiple clients, rather than being employed by a single company. This allows for flexibility in terms of work hours, location, and the type of work undertaken. Remote work, on the other hand, involves working for a single employer but from a location outside of the company's office, often from home or a co-working space.

Both freelancing and remote work opportunities have become increasingly popular in recent years due to advancements in technology, which have made it easier to communicate and collaborate with others from a distance. This has opened up a wide range of possibilities for individuals to pursue their careers while maintaining a better work-life balance. It also allows companies to access a global talent pool and reduce costs associated with maintaining a physical office space.

For freelancers, the ability to work remotely means they can take on projects from clients anywhere in the world, expanding their potential for work and income. They have the freedom to set their own schedules and choose the projects that align with their skills and interests. This can lead to a more fulfilling and varied career, as well as the potential for higher earnings.

Remote work opportunities offer similar benefits, allowing employees to have more control over their schedules and work environments. This can lead to increased job satisfaction and productivity, as well as reduced stress from commuting and office politics. Remote work also opens up opportunities for individuals who may have difficulty accessing traditional office settings, such as those with disabilities or care-giving responsibilities.

However, freelancing and remote work also present unique challenges. For freelancers, there is the need to constantly source new projects and clients, as well as manage the administrative aspects of running a business, such as invoicing and taxes. Remote employees may struggle with feelings of isolation and the blurring of boundaries between work and personal life when working from home.

Overall, freelancing and remote work opportunities offer a new way of approaching work that prioritizes flexibility, autonomy, and work-life balance. As technology continues to advance, it is likely that these opportunities will only continue to grow, providing more individuals with the chance to design their ideal work situations.

To make money through freelancing and remote work opportunities, you can follow these steps:

Identify Your Skills: Determine the skills you possess that are in demand in the freelance market, such as writing, graphic design, programming, digital marketing, etc. Identifying your skills for freelancing involves recognizing your strengths, expertise, and capabilities that are valuable in the freelance marketplace. Here are some steps to help you identify and showcase your skills for freelancing:

Before starting a freelancing job, it's important to identify your main skills in order to effectively market yourself and attract potential clients. One way to identify your main skills is to take an inventory of your past experiences, both professional and personal, and identify the skills that you have used and developed in those experiences. This can include technical skills such as programming, graphic design, or writing, as well as soft skills such as communication, problem-solving, and time management.

Another way to identify your main skills is to ask for feedback from colleagues, friends, or mentors. They may be able to provide insight into your strengths and areas where you excel. Additionally, you can take online assessments or quizzes that are designed to help identify your strengths and skills.

It's also important to consider the skills that are in demand in the freelancing market. Researching the current trends and needs in your industry can help you identify which skills are most valuable and sought after by potential clients. This can help you focus on developing and marketing those skills to stand out in a competitive market.

Once you have identified your main skills, it's important to showcase them in your freelancing profile or portfolio. Highlighting specific examples of how you have used these skills in past projects can provide evidence of your abilities to potential clients. Additionally, consider obtaining certifications or taking additional courses to further develop and enhance your main skills, making you even more attractive to potential clients.

Overall, identifying your main skills before starting a freelancing job is crucial for positioning yourself as a competitive and valuable freelancer. By understanding your strengths and focusing on developing and showcasing those skills, you can increase your chances of success in the freelancing market.

Self-Assessment: Take time to assess your skills, knowledge, and experience. Consider your professional background, education, certifications, and any specialized training you may have received.

Self-assessing for a freelancing job is an important step in ensuring that you are prepared to take on the responsibilities and challenges that come with working independently. To begin with, it's essential to evaluate your skills and expertise in your chosen field. Consider your strengths and weaknesses, and determine how they align with the requirements of the freelancing job you are interested in. This may involve assessing your technical abilities, creativity, problem-solving skills, communication skills, and time management.

In addition to evaluating your skills, it's crucial to assess your level of experience and knowledge in the specific industry or niche you are targeting. Reflect on your past projects, successes, and areas for improvement. This can help you identify gaps in your knowledge or experience that you may need to address before pursuing certain freelancing opportunities.

Furthermore, self-assessment for a freelancing job involves understanding your personal work preferences and habits. Consider your preferred work environment, working hours, and ability to manage your workload independently. Assess your motivation, self-discipline, and ability to stay focused and productive without direct supervision. Understanding these factors can help you determine if freelancing is a suitable career choice for you and if you are ready to take on the responsibilities of working autonomously.

Moreover, it's important to assess your financial readiness for freelancing. Evaluate your current financial situation, including your savings, expenses, and any financial commitments. Consider the potential fluctuations in income that come with freelancing and assess whether you have a financial cushion to support you during lean periods. Additionally, consider the costs associated with setting up and running a freelance business, such as equipment, software, marketing, and professional development.

Another aspect of self-assessment for freelancing involves evaluating your networking and marketing skills. Assess your ability to promote your services, build professional relationships, and market yourself effectively to potential clients. This may involve evaluating your online presence, networking abilities, and knowledge of marketing strategies relevant to freelancers in your industry.

Furthermore, it's essential to assess your risk tolerance and ability to handle uncertainty as a freelancer. Consider how comfortable you are with the variability of income, the potential for project rejections, and the need to continuously adapt to market changes. Assess your ability to handle stress, setbacks, and the need to constantly seek new opportunities.

Lastly, self-assessment for freelancing should involve evaluating your long-term career goals and aspirations. Consider whether freelancing aligns with your professional objectives and whether it offers the opportunities for growth and fulfilment that you seek. Assess whether you have a clear vision for your freelance career and whether you are prepared to invest the time and effort required to achieve your goals.

In conclusion, self-assessing for a freelancing job is a comprehensive process that involves evaluating your skills, experience, work preferences, financial readiness, networking abilities, risk tolerance, and long-term career goals. By conducting a thorough self-assessment, you can gain valuable insights into your readiness for freelancing and identify areas for improvement or further development. This can ultimately help you make informed decisions about pursuing freelancing opportunities and positioning yourself for success in the freelance industry.

Identify Core Skills:

In freelancing, there are several core skills that are essential for success. First and foremost, strong communication skills are crucial. This includes the ability to clearly and effectively communicate with clients, understand their needs, and manage expectations. Additionally, being able to negotiate terms, discuss project details, and provide updates in a timely manner is important for building trust and maintaining good relationships.

Time management is another key skill in freelancing. Freelancers often work on multiple projects with different deadlines, so the ability to prioritize tasks, meet deadlines, and manage workload effectively is critical. This also includes being able to set realistic timelines for project completion and deliver high-quality work within those timeframes.

Technical skills specific to the type of freelancing work are also essential. Whether it's graphic design, web development, writing, or any other specialized field, freelancers need to have a strong grasp of the tools and technologies required for their work. Continuous learning and staying updated with industry trends and best practices is important for maintaining a competitive edge.

Marketing and self-promotion skills are vital for freelancers to attract new clients and projects. This includes creating a strong personal brand, building a professional portfolio, networking with potential clients, and effectively showcasing expertise and past work. Being able to pitch services, write compelling proposals, and sell oneself effectively is crucial for securing new opportunities.

Financial management is an often overlooked but crucial skill for freelancers. This includes setting rates that reflect the value of the work, managing income and expenses, invoicing clients, and handling taxes and other financial aspects of running a freelance business.

Lastly, adaptability and resilience are important skills for freelancers. The ability to quickly adapt to new projects, client expectations, and industry changes is essential. Freelancers also need to be resilient in the face of rejection, setbacks, and challenges that are inherent in the freelancing world.

Overall, freelancing requires a combination of technical expertise, business acumen, communication skills, and personal attributes to succeed in a competitive and dynamic

environment. Mastering these core skills can help freelancers thrive and build a successful career in the gig economy.

Identify your core skills and competencies, such as project management, graphic design, web development, writing, marketing, data analysis, customer service, or any other areas where you excel.

How to identify core skills before doing freelancing:

Identifying core skills before venturing into freelancing is crucial for success in the competitive market. Start by assessing your strengths and weaknesses, and consider the skills that you excel at. These could include technical skills such as programming, graphic design, writing, or marketing, as well as soft skills like communication, time management, and problem-solving. Reflect on your previous work experiences, educational background, and personal interests to pinpoint areas where you have a natural talent or a strong passion. Additionally, research the current demand in the freelancing market to identify which skills are highly sought after. Look at job postings, industry trends, and networking with other freelancers to gain insights into the most valuable skills. It's also beneficial to seek feedback from mentors, colleagues, or industry professionals to gain an outside perspective on your strengths and areas for improvement. Once you have identified your core skills, focus on honing and developing them further through online courses, workshops, or practical experience. Building a strong foundation of core skills will not only make you more marketable as a freelancer but also increase your confidence and ability to deliver high-quality work to your clients.

Soft Skills: Soft skills in freelancing are essential for success in the competitive and dynamic world of remote work. These skills are not specific to any particular job or industry, but rather are the personal attributes and qualities that enable freelancers to effectively interact with clients, manage their time and workload, and thrive in a constantly changing work environment.

Communication is perhaps the most crucial soft skill for freelancers. Clear and effective communication with clients, colleagues, and other stakeholders is essential for understanding project requirements, providing updates on progress, and resolving any issues that may arise. Freelancers must be able to express themselves clearly and professionally through written communication, such as emails and messages, as well as verbal communication during phone or video calls.

Time management and organization are also vital soft skills for freelancers. With multiple projects and deadlines to juggle, freelancers must be able to prioritize tasks, set realistic timelines, and manage their workload efficiently. This requires strong organizational skills to keep track of project details, deadlines, and client requirements, as well as the ability to stay focused and productive while working independently.

Adaptability is another important soft skill for freelancers. The nature of freelance work often means dealing with unexpected changes, shifting priorities, and new challenges on a regular basis. Freelancers must be able to adapt to these changes quickly and effectively, whether it's adjusting to new project requirements, accommodating client feedback, or learning new tools and technologies to stay competitive in their field.

Problem-solving and critical thinking are also valuable soft skills for freelancers. When faced with complex projects or unexpected obstacles, freelancers must be able to analyze the situation, identify potential solutions, and make informed decisions to move the project forward. This may involve creative thinking, resourcefulness, and the ability to think outside the box to find innovative solutions to problems.

Collaboration and teamwork are important soft skills for freelancers who often work with clients, other freelancers, or in virtual teams. Being able to collaborate effectively, share ideas, provide constructive feedback, and work towards common goals is essential for delivering high-quality work and building strong professional relationships.

Finally, self-motivation and resilience are critical soft skills for freelancers. Working independently requires a high level of self-discipline, motivation, and the ability to stay focused and productive without direct supervision. Freelancers also need to be resilient in the face of rejection, setbacks, or periods of uncertainty, as freelancing often involves navigating a fluctuating workload and income.

In conclusion, soft skills play a crucial role in the success of freelancers. By honing their communication, time management, adaptability, problem-solving, collaboration, and self-motivation skills, freelancers can not only deliver exceptional work but also build a strong reputation in the competitive freelance market. Don't overlook soft skills such as communication, problem-solving, time management, teamwork, adaptability, and critical thinking. These skills are highly valued in the freelance world.

Specialized Skills: Specialized skills in freelancing encompass a wide range of expertise that cater to specific industries and niche markets. These skills are highly sought after by clients looking for top-tier talent to fulfil their project requirements. Some of the specialized skills in freelancing include but are not limited to:

1. Web Development: Freelancers with expertise in web development possess skills in programming languages such as HTML, CSS, JavaScript, and PHP. They are adept at creating responsive and visually appealing websites that are optimized for user experience and functionality.

2. Graphic Design: Freelancers specializing in graphic design have a keen eye for aesthetics and the ability to create visually stunning designs for branding, marketing collateral, and digital media. They are proficient in design software such as Adobe Photoshop, Illustrator, and InDesign.

3. Content Writing: Freelancers with specialized skills in content writing are adept at creating engaging and compelling written content for various platforms including websites, blogs, social media, and marketing materials. They possess strong writing skills, a good understanding of SEO, and the ability to tailor content to specific target audiences.

4. Digital Marketing: Freelancers specializing in digital marketing have expertise in areas such as search engine optimization (SEO), social media marketing, email marketing, and pay-per-click advertising. They are skilled at developing and implementing digital marketing strategies to drive traffic, generate leads, and increase brand awareness.

5. Mobile App Development: Freelancers with specialized skills in mobile app development are proficient in programming languages such as Java, Swift, and Kotlin. They have the ability to create functional and user-friendly mobile applications for iOS and Android platforms.

6. Video Production: Freelancers specializing in video production possess skills in videography, video editing, and motion graphics. They are capable of producing high-quality video content for various purposes including marketing campaigns, tutorials, and brand storytelling.

7. E-commerce Development: Freelancers with expertise in e-commerce development have a deep understanding of platforms such as Shopify, WooCommerce, and Magento. They are skilled at creating and customizing online stores that are secure, user-friendly, and optimized for sales.

8. Data Analysis: Freelancers specializing in data analysis possess strong analytical skills and proficiency in tools such as Microsoft Excel, SQL, and Tableau. They are capable of interpreting data, creating visualizations, and deriving valuable insights to support business decision-making.

9. Virtual Assistance: Freelancers with specialized skills in virtual assistance are proficient in administrative tasks such as scheduling, email management, customer support, and data entry. They possess strong organizational skills and the ability to handle multiple tasks efficiently.

10. Cybersecurity: Freelancers specializing in cybersecurity possess expertise in areas such as network security, information security, and ethical hacking. They are capable of assessing security risks, implementing protective measures, and ensuring the integrity of digital assets.

These specialized skills enable freelancers to offer high-quality services that cater to specific client needs, making them valuable assets in the freelance marketplace. By honing their expertise in these specialized areas, freelancers can differentiate themselves from the competition and build a strong reputation within their respective industries. If you have specialized skills or unique expertise in a niche area, such as blockchain technology, machine learning, cybersecurity, or industry-specific knowledge, highlight these as well.

Portfolio Development: Developing a portfolio in freelancing jobs involves several key steps to showcase your skills and experience to potential clients. First, identify your specific areas of expertise within freelancing, such as graphic design, writing, web development, or digital marketing. Once you have a clear focus, start by gathering examples of your work that best represent your abilities. This can include samples of previous projects, client testimonials, or any relevant certifications or qualifications.

Next, create a professional portfolio website or online profile that highlights your work and provides a brief overview of your skills and experience. Make sure to include a variety of projects that demonstrate your range and versatility as a freelancer. Additionally, consider including case studies or detailed descriptions of your work process to give potential clients insight into how you approach projects.

Networking within the freelancing community can also help you build your portfolio. Connect with other freelancers, join industry-specific groups or forums, and attend relevant events to expand your professional circle and potentially find new opportunities to collaborate on projects. Building relationships with other freelancers can also lead to referrals and recommendations, which can further enhance your portfolio.

As you continue to take on new projects, regularly update your portfolio with your latest work. This not only keeps your portfolio fresh and relevant but also shows potential clients that you are actively working and producing high-quality results. Additionally, consider seeking out feedback from clients to further strengthen your portfolio. Positive testimonials and reviews can help build credibility and trust with potential clients.

Lastly, be strategic about how you present your portfolio to potential clients. Tailor your portfolio to showcase examples of work that align with the specific needs and interests of each client. Highlighting relevant experience and successful projects can help demonstrate your value and expertise in a way that resonates with each individual client.

By following these steps, you can effectively develop a strong portfolio in freelancing jobs that effectively showcases your skills, experience, and professionalism to potential clients. Build a portfolio that showcases your work, projects, and accomplishments. This can include samples of your writing, design work, coding projects, or any other relevant materials that demonstrate your skills.

Client Testimonials: If you have previous freelance experience, gather client testimonials and feedback to highlight your professionalism and the quality of your work. To gather clients' testimonies for your freelancing jobs, there are several effective strategies you can employ. First and foremost, delivering exceptional work and providing top-notch customer service is crucial. Satisfied clients are more likely to provide positive feedback and testimonials. You can also directly ask your clients for their testimonies, explaining how much it would mean to you and your business. Additionally, consider creating a streamlined process for collecting testimonials, such as sending a follow-up email after completing a project with a link to a testimonial submission form. Another approach is to offer an incentive for clients to provide testimonials, such as a discount on future services or a small gift as a token of appreciation. Utilizing social proof by showcasing existing client testimonials on your website and social media platforms can also encourage new clients to leave their own feedback. Finally, consider reaching out to past clients for testimonials, as their experiences can also speak to the quality of your work. By implementing these strategies, you can effectively gather clients' testimonies for your freelancing jobs and enhance your professional reputation.

Networking and Recommendations: Networking is the practice of making connections and building relationships with professionals in your industry. In the context of freelancing, networking is essential for finding new clients, collaborating with other freelancers, and staying up to date with industry trends. There are several ways to network as a freelancer, including attending industry events and conferences, joining online communities and forums, and reaching out to potential clients or collaborators through social media or professional networking platforms like LinkedIn.

When it comes to recommendations for freelancing, there are a few key points to keep in mind. First and foremost, it's important to have a strong online presence. This includes having a professional website or portfolio to showcase your work, as well as maintaining active profiles on relevant social media platforms. This can help potential clients find and learn more about you, and can also help you connect with other professionals in your field.

Another important recommendation for freelancers is to always deliver high-quality work and excellent customer service. Satisfied clients are more likely to recommend you to others and to hire you for future projects. Building a strong reputation for reliability and professionalism can lead to repeat business and referrals, which are invaluable for freelancers.

In addition, it's important for freelancers to be proactive in seeking out new opportunities. This can include reaching out to potential clients directly, applying for freelance gigs on job boards or freelancing platforms, and seeking out collaborations with other freelancers or businesses. Being proactive and persistent in pursuing new opportunities can help freelancers build a steady client base and a diverse portfolio of work.

Finally, it's important for freelancers to stay organized and manage their time effectively. This includes setting clear goals for their freelance business, keeping track of deadlines and deliverables, and managing their finances responsibly. By staying organized and disciplined, freelancers can ensure that they are able to meet their clients' needs and maintain a successful freelance career.

Overall, networking and recommendations for freelancing are essential for building a successful freelance career. By building strong connections with other professionals, maintaining a strong online presence, delivering high-quality work, being proactive in seeking out new opportunities, and staying organized, freelancers can build a thriving freelance business and achieve long-term success in their industry.

Leverage your professional network to seek recommendations or referrals from colleagues, mentors, or former employers. Recommendations can add credibility to your skills and expertise.

Continuous Learning: Continuous learning in freelancing refers to the ongoing process of acquiring new knowledge, skills, and expertise to stay relevant and competitive in the ever-evolving freelance market. As a freelancer, it is essential to continuously update and expand your skill set to meet the changing demands of clients and industry trends. This involves staying abreast of the latest technologies, tools, and best practices in your field, as well as seeking out opportunities for professional development and training.

Continuous learning in freelancing also encompasses the need to adapt to new challenges and opportunities that arise in the gig economy. This may involve learning new project management techniques, honing your communication and negotiation skills, or familiarizing yourself with different project management tools and platforms. Additionally, freelancers must stay informed about changes in regulations, tax laws, and industry standards that may impact their work.

Embracing continuous learning as a freelancer also means being open to feedback and seeking out opportunities for mentorship and networking. Engaging with other professionals in your field can provide valuable insights and perspectives that can help you grow and improve as a freelancer. Seeking feedback from clients and peers can also help you identify areas for improvement and refine your approach to delivering high-quality work.

Moreover, continuous learning in freelancing involves cultivating a growth mindset and a willingness to take on new challenges. This may involve stepping out of your comfort zone to explore new niches or industries, taking on projects that push your boundaries, or experimenting with different approaches to your work. Embracing a mindset of continuous learning can help freelancers adapt to change, overcome obstacles, and seize new opportunities for professional growth.

In conclusion, continuous learning is a fundamental aspect of freelancing that empowers individuals to adapt, grow, and thrive in a dynamic and competitive market. By staying curious, open-minded, and proactive about acquiring new knowledge and skills, freelancers can position themselves for long-term success and fulfilment in their careers.

Stay updated with industry trends and advancements in your field. Continuous learning through courses, workshops, and certifications can enhance your skill set and make you more competitive as a freelancer.

Online Profiles: To create professional profiles on freelancing platforms and social media networks that emphasize your skills and expertise, it is important to start with a strong and compelling summary or bio. This should include a brief overview of your professional background, highlighting key skills, experiences, and accomplishments. Use keywords relevant to your industry to optimize your profile for search engines and make it easier for potential clients or employers to find you.

When it comes to showcasing your skills, consider including a portfolio of your work, such as samples, projects, or case studies that demonstrate your expertise. This can provide tangible evidence of your abilities and help build credibility with potential clients.

In addition, be sure to list your specific skills and areas of expertise in a clear and organized manner. Use bullet points or short paragraphs to highlight your strengths and capabilities. You may also want to consider including any relevant certifications, licenses, or professional affiliations to further validate your expertise.

Another important aspect of creating a professional profile is to gather recommendations or endorsements from previous clients, colleagues, or supervisors. These testimonials can add credibility to your profile and provide social proof of your skills and professionalism.

It's also important to maintain an active and engaging presence on these platforms by regularly sharing updates, insights, or relevant content related to your industry. This can help position you as a thought leader and expert in your field, further emphasizing your skills and expertise.

Lastly, be sure to keep your profiles up to date with any new skills, experiences, or accomplishments. This shows that you are continuously growing and evolving in your career, which can be attractive to potential clients or employers. By following these tips, you can create professional profiles that effectively highlight your skills and expertises, ultimately helping you stand out in a competitive freelancing and social media landscape. Use keywords relevant to your skills to improve visibility in search results.

Join Freelance Platforms: Joining freelancing platforms can significantly enhance your freelancing performance in several ways. First and foremost, these platforms provide a vast marketplace where you can showcase your skills and expertise to a wide range of potential clients. By creating a profile and portfolio on these platforms, you can effectively market yourself and attract clients who are seeking the services you offer. This exposure can lead to a steady stream of work opportunities, allowing you to build a strong client base and establish a solid reputation within your industry.

Moreover, freelancing platforms often offer various tools and resources to help freelancers manage their projects more efficiently. From time-tracking and invoicing tools to communication and file-sharing capabilities, these platforms can streamline the administrative aspects of freelancing, allowing you to focus more on delivering high-quality work to your clients. Additionally, many freelancing platforms provide dispute resolution mechanisms and secure payment systems, which can help protect you from potential payment issues and conflicts with clients.

Furthermore, joining freelancing platforms can also provide valuable networking opportunities. By interacting with other freelancers and industry professionals on these platforms, you can gain insights, advice, and support from peers who understand the challenges and opportunities of freelancing. This sense of community can be invaluable for staying motivated, learning new skills, and staying updated on industry trends.

In addition, many freelancing platforms offer educational resources and training programs to help freelancers enhance their skills and expand their knowledge. Whether it's through webinars, tutorials, or online courses, these platforms can provide valuable learning opportunities that can help you stay competitive in your field and take your freelancing career to the next level.

Finally, freelancing platforms can also offer a level of credibility and legitimacy to your freelancing business. By being associated with reputable platforms that have established themselves in the industry, you can build trust with potential clients who may be more inclined to hire freelancers who are part of these platforms. This association can enhance your professional image and give clients the confidence that they are working with a reliable and trustworthy freelancer.

In conclusion, joining freelancing platforms can be a game-changer for your freelancing performance. From increasing your visibility and attracting clients to providing essential tools and resources, these platforms can empower you to take your freelancing career to new heights. Whether you're just starting out as a freelancer or looking to grow your existing business, leveraging the opportunities offered by freelancing platforms can be an effective strategy for success in the gig economy. Sign up on freelance platforms such as Upwork, Freelancer, Fiverr, and others. Create a compelling profile that highlights your skills and experience.

Apply for Projects: To apply for projects on freelancing platforms, you first need to create a strong profile that showcases your skills, experience, and expertise. This includes a professional headshot, a compelling bio that highlights your strengths and experience, and a portfolio of your best work. Once your profile is complete, you can start browsing projects that match your skills and interests. When you find a project that you're interested in, take the time to carefully read the project description and requirements. Tailor your proposal to show the client that you understand their needs and are the best person for the job. Highlight relevant experience, provide examples of similar projects you've completed successfully, and explain how you plan to approach the project. Be sure to include a clear and competitive bid that reflects the value you will bring to the client. Finally, submit your proposal and be prepared to respond to any questions or requests for additional information from the client. Keep in mind that competition can be fierce, so it's important to make sure your proposal stands out by being professional, thorough, and tailored to the specific project. With a strong profile and well-crafted proposals, you can increase your chances of landing projects on freelancing platforms.

Deliver Quality Work: Delivering high-quality work for clients' requests in freelancing requires a combination of skills, professionalism, and attention to detail. To start, it's important to thoroughly understand the client's requirements and expectations. This involves asking clarifying questions, seeking examples or references, and ensuring that you have a clear understanding of the project scope. Communication is key in this process, as it helps to avoid misunderstandings and ensures that you and the client are on the same page.

Once you have a solid understanding of the client's needs, it's essential to plan your work effectively. This includes setting realistic timelines, breaking down the project into manageable tasks, and allocating resources appropriately. Time management is crucial in freelancing, as it allows you to meet deadlines and deliver quality work without unnecessary stress.

When it comes to actually completing the work, attention to detail is paramount. Whether it's writing, design, coding, or any other type of freelancing work, taking the time to review your work for errors, inconsistencies, or areas for improvement can make a significant difference in the quality of your output. This may involve proofreading, testing, or seeking feedback from peers or mentors.

In addition to attention to detail, it's important to continuously strive for improvement in your skills and knowledge. This can involve staying updated on industry trends, learning new tools or techniques, and seeking feedback from clients to understand how you can better meet their needs. Professional development is an ongoing process that can help you deliver high-quality work consistently.

Finally, professionalism in all aspects of your freelancing work is crucial for delivering high-quality results. This includes maintaining clear and respectful communication with clients, being transparent about your process and any potential challenges, and handling revisions or feedback in a constructive manner. Building a reputation for professionalism can lead to repeat business and referrals, which are valuable assets in the freelancing world.

In summary, delivering high-quality work for clients' requests in freelancing requires a combination of understanding client needs, effective planning, attention to detail, continuous improvement, and professionalism. By focusing on these areas, you can consistently meet and exceed client expectations, leading to successful and satisfying freelancing experiences

Expand Your Network: Expanding your network on freelancing platforms can be crucial for finding new opportunities and growing your business. Here are a few strategies to help you expand your network:

1. Optimize your profile: Make sure your profile on freelancing platforms is complete and showcases your skills, experience, and portfolio. Use keywords relevant to your expertise to make it easier for potential clients to find you.

2. Engage with the community: Actively participate in forums, groups, and discussions within freelancing platforms. Offer advice, share your experiences, and connect with other freelancers. Engaging with the community can help you build relationships and establish yourself as an expert in your field.

3. Attend networking events: Many freelancing platforms host networking events, webinars, and workshops. Take advantage of these opportunities to meet other freelancers, potential clients, and industry experts. Networking events can provide valuable insights and connections that can help you expand your network.

4. Reach out to past clients: Keep in touch with past clients and ask for referrals or testimonials. Satisfied clients can be a great source of new business and can help you expand your network through word-of-mouth recommendations.

5. Collaborate with other freelancers: Consider collaborating with other freelancers on projects or referring clients to each other. Building relationships with other freelancers can lead to new opportunities and help you expand your network within the freelancing community.

6. Leverage social media: Use social media platforms to connect with potential clients, industry influencers, and other freelancers. Share your work, engage with relevant content, and participate in conversations to expand your online presence and network.

7. Offer value: Provide valuable content, resources, or insights related to your expertise. This can help you attract potential clients and establish yourself as a knowledgeable and trustworthy freelancer within your industry.

By implementing these strategies, you can expand your network on freelancing platforms and increase your chances of finding new opportunities, building relationships, and growing your business.

Manage Finances: Managing finances while doing freelancing jobs requires careful planning and discipline. Freelancing often comes with irregular income, so it's important to create a budget and stick to it. Start by tracking your income and expenses to get a clear picture of your financial situation. This will help you identify areas where you can cut costs and save money.

It's also important to set aside money for taxes. As a freelancer, you are responsible for paying your own taxes, so it's crucial to save a portion of your income for this purpose. Consider working with a tax professional to ensure that you are setting aside the right amount and taking advantage of any deductions or credits available to you.

In addition to saving for taxes, it's a good idea to build an emergency fund. Since freelancing income can be unpredictable, having a financial cushion can provide peace of mind and help you weather any unexpected expenses or periods of low income.

When it comes to managing your income, consider setting up separate bank accounts for different purposes. For example, you might have one account for business income and expenses, another for taxes, and another for personal expenses. This can help you keep your finances organized and make it easier to track your cash flow.

In terms of expenses, it's important to be mindful of your spending. Look for ways to cut costs, such as negotiating lower rates with service providers or finding more affordable alternatives for things like software subscriptions or office supplies. It's also important to prioritize your spending and focus on the things that are essential for your business and personal well-being.

As a freelancer, it's also important to think about retirement savings. Unlike traditional employees who may have access to employer-sponsored retirement plans, freelancers are responsible for setting up their own retirement accounts. Consider working with a financial advisor to explore options such as individual retirement accounts (IRAs) or solo 401(k) plans.

In addition to saving for retirement, consider investing in your professional development. This might include taking courses or attending conferences to improve your skills and expand your network. By investing in yourself, you can position yourself for long-term success as a freelancer.

Another important aspect of managing finances as a freelancer is invoicing and getting paid; make adequate sure you have clear contracts in place with your clients that outline payment terms and expectations. Consider using invoicing software to streamline the process and make it easier to track payments. It's also important to follow up on late payments and have a plan in place for dealing with clients who are slow to pay.

Consider working with a financial advisor or accountant who has experience working with freelancers. They can provide valuable guidance and help you navigate the unique financial challenges that come with freelancing. By staying organized, being proactive about saving and budgeting, and seeking professional advice when needed, you can set yourself up for financial success as a freelancer.

Explore Remote Job Opportunities:

Remote job opportunities refer to employment opportunities that allow individuals to work from a location outside of a traditional office setting. These opportunities have become increasingly prevalent in recent years, thanks to advancements in technology that enable seamless communication and collaboration regardless of physical location. Remote job opportunities can take many forms, including full-time, part-time, freelance, and contract positions across a wide range of industries and professions.

One of the most common types of remote job opportunities is telecommuting, where employees work from home or another remote location for all or part of their workweek. This arrangement offers flexibility and convenience for employees, as well as potential cost savings for employers who may be able to reduce their office space and overhead expenses. Telecommuting roles can span various fields, including customer service, sales, marketing, writing, design, programming, and more.

Another popular form of remote job opportunities is freelancing or independent contracting. Many professionals, such as graphic designers, web developers, writers, and consultants, choose to work independently and take on projects from clients on a remote basis. This allows them to have greater control over their schedules, choose the projects they are passionate about, and potentially earn higher rates than they would in traditional employment.

In addition to telecommuting and freelancing, remote job opportunities also encompass virtual positions within traditional companies. Many organizations now offer remote work options for certain roles, allowing employees to collaborate with colleagues and contribute to projects from anywhere with an internet connection. This arrangement can be particularly beneficial for individuals who live in areas with limited job opportunities or who require flexibility due to personal circumstances.

The rise of remote job opportunities has opened up new possibilities for individuals who may not be able to work in a traditional office environment due to health concerns, caregiving responsibilities, or geographic constraints. It also benefits employers by widening the talent pool and enabling them to access skilled professionals from diverse locations. Additionally, remote work can contribute to a better work-life balance for employees, as it eliminates commuting time and allows for greater flexibility in managing personal and professional commitments.

Remote job opportunities are not limited to specific industries or professions. With the right skills and resources, individuals can find remote work in fields such as education, healthcare, finance, technology, creative arts, and more. The key is to leverage technology tools for communication and project management, cultivate strong time management and self-discipline skills, and stay proactive in seeking out remote job opportunities through online job boards, networking, and professional organizations.

While remote job opportunities offer numerous benefits, they also come with unique challenges. Working remotely requires self-motivation, effective communication skills, and the ability to manage time and tasks independently. It can also be isolating at times, especially for individuals who thrive on social interaction and collaboration. However, with the right strategies and support systems in place, many people find that remote work offers the perfect balance of autonomy and connection.

If you are looking for remote job opportunities online, there are plenty of options available in today's digital age. Many companies are now offering remote positions that allow employees to work from the comfort of their own homes. Some common examples of remote job opportunities include roles in customer service, data entry, virtual assistance, software development, graphic design, digital marketing, content writing, and online tutoring. Additionally, there are opportunities for remote positions in fields such as finance, healthcare, education, and project management. With the increasing demand for remote work, more and more companies are embracing this flexible work arrangement, making it easier than ever to find remote job opportunities online. Whether you are looking for a full-time remote position or a part-time gig, there are numerous websites and job boards dedicated to connecting remote workers with employers offering virtual job opportunities. Working remotely can offer a great work-life balance and the flexibility to work from anywhere with an internet connection. If you are considering a remote job, be sure to research the company and position thoroughly to ensure it is the right fit for you. With the abundance of remote job opportunities available online, you are sure to find a role that aligns with your skills and interests.

In conclusion, remote job opportunities are a growing and diverse segment of the modern workforce. Whether it's telecommuting, freelancing, or virtual employment within a traditional company, remote work offers flexibility, convenience, and potential for career growth. As technology continues to evolve and organizations embrace remote work models, the landscape of job opportunities will continue to expand, providing individuals with more options to pursue fulfilling careers while maintaining the lifestyle that best suits their needs.

Chapter 3
Starting a Drop-shipping Business:

Dropshipping is a retail fulfilment method where a store doesn't keep the products it sells in stock. Instead, when a store sells a product using the dropshipping model, it purchases the item from a third party and has it shipped directly to the customer. As a result, the merchant never sees or handles the product. The biggest difference between dropshipping and the standard retail model is that the selling merchant doesn't stock or own inventory. Instead, the merchant purchases inventory as needed from a third party – usually a wholesaler or manufacturer – to fulfil orders.

One of the key benefits of dropshipping is that it eliminates the need for a physical storefront. This means that sellers can start a business without having to invest in inventory up front, making it an attractive option for entrepreneurs who want to start an online store but don't have a lot of capital to work with. Additionally, because the seller doesn't have to handle the products, they can operate their business from anywhere with an internet connection. This flexibility allows for a more mobile lifestyle and can be particularly appealing to digital nomads and those who value location independence.

Another advantage of dropshipping is that it allows sellers to offer a wide variety of products without having to deal with the complexity of managing inventory. This means that sellers can quickly test different products and niches to see what resonates with their target audience, without having to commit to large quantities of stock. By being able to easily add or remove products from their online store, sellers can adapt to changing market trends and customer preferences with minimal risk.

In addition, dropshipping can be a cost-effective way for sellers to enter new markets or expand their product offerings. With traditional retail models, entering a new market often involves significant upfront costs, such as setting up distribution channels and securing inventory. However, with dropshipping, sellers can quickly and relatively easily add new products to their store without having to make major financial commitments.

However, dropshipping also has its challenges. One of the main drawbacks is that sellers have less control over the fulfilment process. Since they rely on third-party suppliers to ship products directly to customers, sellers are at the mercy of those suppliers when it comes to shipping times, product availability, and overall quality. This can lead to issues such as delayed shipments, backordered items, and inconsistent product quality, which can negatively impact the seller's reputation and customer satisfaction.

Another potential challenge with dropshipping is that it can be more difficult for sellers to differentiate themselves from competitors. Because many dropshipping suppliers offer the same or similar products, sellers may find it challenging to stand out in a crowded market. This can lead to price competition and margin erosion, as sellers are forced to lower prices in order to remain competitive.

Furthermore, because sellers don't have control over inventory, they are also at risk of selling products that are out of stock or discontinued by their suppliers. This can lead to frustrating experiences for customers who have placed orders only to be informed later that the product is no longer available. Managing customer expectations and dealing with potential backlash from these situations can be a significant challenge for dropshipping sellers.

Despite these challenges, dropshipping continues to be a popular business model for many online entrepreneurs. Its low barrier to entry, flexibility, and potential for cost savings make it an attractive option for those looking to start an e-commerce business. However, success in dropshipping requires careful planning, strong relationships with reliable suppliers, and a focus on providing excellent customer service to overcome the inherent challenges of the model.

Dropshipping comes in various forms, each with its own unique characteristics and benefits. One type of dropshipping is traditional dropshipping, where a retailer sources products from a supplier and fulfils orders directly to the customer. This type of dropshipping allows retailers to offer a wide range of products without having to hold inventory or manage shipping logistics.

Another type of dropshipping is print-on-demand dropshipping, where retailers partner with a print-on-demand supplier to create custom products such as t-shirts, mugs, and phone cases. When a customer places an order, the product is then printed and shipped directly from the supplier to the customer. This type of dropshipping is popular for retailers looking to offer unique, customizable products without the need for large upfront investments.

Additionally, there is also wholesale dropshipping, where retailers work with wholesale suppliers to dropship products in bulk. This allows retailers to benefit from lower wholesale prices while still enjoying the convenience of not having to hold inventory or manage shipping.

Furthermore, there is also private label dropshipping, where retailers work with manufacturers to create custom-branded products. This allows retailers to differentiate themselves in the market and build brand loyalty without the need for large production runs or inventory storage.

Lastly, there is also automated dropshipping, where retailers use software and tools to automate various aspects of their dropshipping business, such as product sourcing, order fulfillment, and customer service. This type of dropshipping can help retailers streamline their operations and scale their business more efficiently.

In conclusion, the various types of dropshipping offer retailers different ways to source and fulfil products, each with its own set of advantages and considerations. Whether it's traditional dropshipping, print-on-demand, wholesale, private label, or automated dropshipping, retailers have the flexibility to choose the approach that best aligns with their business goals and target market.

When selecting a niche for dropshipping, it's important to consider a few key factors in order to maximize your chances of success. First and foremost, it's essential to choose a niche that you are passionate about and have a genuine interest in. This will not only make the process more enjoyable for you, but it will also give you a competitive edge as you will be more knowledgeable and enthusiastic about the products you are selling. Additionally, consider the profitability of the niche. Look for products that have a high demand but low competition, as this will increase your chances of making sales and generating a healthy profit margin. Conduct thorough market research to identify trends and potential opportunities within different niches. It's also important to consider the target audience for your chosen niche. Think about whom your ideal customers are and what their needs and preferences are likely to be. This will help you tailor your marketing efforts and product selection to better appeal to your target market. Furthermore, consider the logistics of sourcing and shipping products within your chosen niche. Look for suppliers who offer high-quality products at competitive prices and who can reliably fulfil orders in a timely manner. Finally, consider the long-term potential of the niche. While it's important to capitalize on current trends, it's also wise to choose a niche with staying power and potential for growth in the future. By carefully considering these factors and conducting thorough research, you can select a niche that is well-suited to your interests, profitable, and has the potential for long-term success in the world of dropshipping.

Droppshipping is profitable when there is progressive increase in the demand of the items.

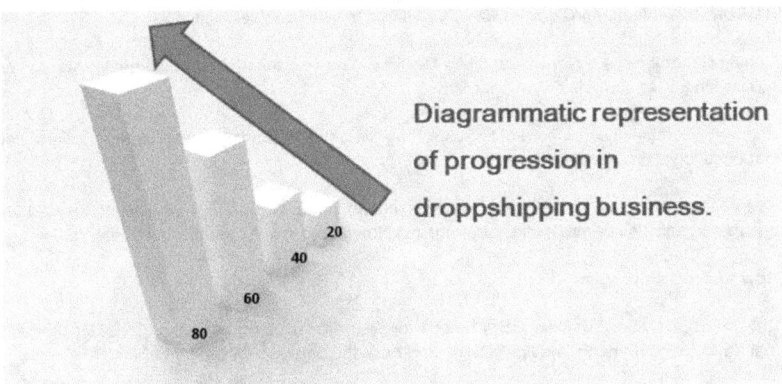

Diagrammatic representation of progression in droppshipping business.

In droppshipping, the seller (the dropshipper) partners with a supplier or wholesaler who offers dropshipping services.
The seller lists the supplier's products on their online store or platform at retail prices.
When a customer places an order for a product, the seller forwards the order and shipment details to the supplier.
The supplier then ships the product directly to the customer, often using the seller's branding and packaging materials.

In essence, the seller acts as an intermediary, marketing and selling product without holding inventory. This allows sellers to focus on marketing, customer service, and sales, without the burden of managing inventory, storage, and fulfilment.

Key benefits of dropshipping include:

Low Start-up Costs: Dropshipping requires minimal upfront investment since there's no need to purchase and store inventory.

Reduced Overhead: Without the need for warehousing and inventory management, overhead costs are significantly lower.

Flexibility: Dropshipping allows sellers to offer a wide range of products without needing to invest in inventory.

However, there are also potential challenges associated with dropshipping, such as:

Lower Profit Margins: Since the seller purchases products at wholesale prices and sells them at retail prices, profit margins can be lower compared to traditional retail models.

Quality Control: Sellers rely on suppliers to fulfil orders and maintain product quality, which can be challenging to control.

Shipping Complexities: Coordinating shipping times and managing multiple suppliers can introduce logistical complexities.

Overall, dropshipping can be an attractive option for entrepreneurs who want to start an e-commerce business with minimal upfront investment and lower operational overhead.

How to drop-ship:

Choose Your Niche: Select a niche market for your dropshipping business. Consider products that have a high demand, are lightweight, and have the potential for profit margins.

Research Suppliers: Find reputable suppliers who offer dropshipping services for the products you want to sell. Consider factors such as product quality, shipping times, and customer service.

Set Up an Online Store: Create an e-commerce website using platforms like Shopify, WooCommerce, or Big Commerce. Customize your store to reflect your brand and showcase your products effectively.

Source Products: Add products from your chosen suppliers to your online store. Ensure that you have high-quality product images and detailed descriptions.

Optimize for Conversions: Implement best practices for e-commerce conversion optimization, including clear product descriptions, high-quality images, and a user-friendly checkout process.

Marketing and Promotion: Develop a marketing strategy to drive traffic to your store via paid and unpaid traffic. This can include social media marketing, influencer partnerships, content marketing, and search engine optimization (SEO).

Customer Service: Provide excellent customer service to build trust and loyalty. Be responsive to customer inquiries and address any issues promptly.

Order Fulfillment: When a customer places an order, notify your supplier to ship the product directly to the customer. Ensure that the shipping process is smooth and reliable.

Analyze and Adjust: Regularly analyze your sales data, customer feedback, and website performance to make informed decisions about your product offerings and marketing strategies.

Scale Your Business: As your business grows, consider expanding your product line, optimizing your operations, and exploring new marketing channels.

By following these steps, you can start making money through a drop-shipping business.

Chapter 4
Exploring Print-on-Demand Services:

Print-on-demand services have revolutionized the way individuals and businesses approach the production and distribution of printed materials. These services offer a cost-effective and efficient solution for printing books, magazines, brochures, and other materials in small quantities, eliminating the need for large print runs and excessive inventory. With print-on-demand, customers can order as few or as many copies as they need, reducing waste and minimizing the financial risk associated with traditional printing methods. This flexibility also allows for quick updates and revisions to be made to printed materials, ensuring that the most current information is always available. Additionally, print-on-demand services often offer a wide range of customization options, allowing customers to personalize their printed materials with unique designs, layouts, and finishes. This level of customization can help businesses and individuals create professional-looking materials that effectively represent their brand and message. Furthermore, print-on-demand services typically include distribution and fulfillment options, making it easy for customers to have their printed materials shipped directly to their desired locations. This streamlined process saves time and resources, enabling businesses to focus on their core operations without the burden of managing inventory and logistics. Overall, print-on-demand services provide a convenient and sustainable solution for meeting printing needs, offering a range of benefits including cost savings, flexibility, customization, and efficient distribution.

To make money exploring print-on-demand services, follow these steps listed below and explore the advantages of making money through this type of online money making process.
To explore print-on-demand services, you can follow these steps to familiarize yourself with the options available and make informed decisions:

Research Print-on-Demand Providers: Researching print-on-demand service providers involves several key steps to ensure you find the right fit for your needs. First, start by identifying your specific requirements, such as the type of products you want to sell, the volume of sales you anticipate, and any special features or integrations you may need. Once you have a clear understanding of your needs, begin researching different print-on-demand providers. Look for reviews and testimonials from other users to gauge their satisfaction with the service and the quality of the products. It's also important to compare pricing structures; including base costs, shipping fees, and any additional charges for customization or special features.

Next, consider the technical aspects of the print-on-demand service, such as the quality of printing, the range of products offered, and the ease of use of their design tools and interfaces. Some providers may offer more advanced features like mockup generators, branding options, or integrations with e-commerce platforms that can streamline your workflow.

Additionally, take into account the level of customer support and communication offered by each provider. It's crucial to have reliable support when issues arise or when you have questions about the printing process, order fulfilment, or any other aspect of the service.

Furthermore, consider the production and shipping times of each provider. Fast and reliable fulfilment is essential to ensure a positive customer experience and to meet your own business goals.

Finally, don't overlook the importance of the provider's environmental and ethical practices. Many customers are increasingly conscious of the environmental impact of their purchases, so partnering with a print-on-demand service that prioritizes sustainability and ethical production can be a selling point for your business.

By conducting thorough research into these various aspects of print-on-demand service providers, you can make an informed decision that aligns with your business goals and values.
Start by researching different print-on-demand (POD) service providers. Look for reputable companies that offer a range of products, quality printing, and reliable shipping.

Review Product Catalogues: When reviewing product catalogues, it is important to approach the task with a systematic and thorough method. The first step is to familiarize yourself with the layout and organization of the catalogue. This may involve browsing through the different sections and categories to get a sense of the range of products available. Take note of how the products are grouped together and any special features or promotions that are highlighted.

Next, it is important to carefully examine the individual product listings. Pay attention to the details provided for each item, such as the product name, description, specifications, and pricing. Look for any inconsistencies or inaccuracies in the information provided, as these can impact the overall quality of the catalogue.

As you review each product, consider how well it is presented in terms of visual appeal. This includes assessing the quality of any images or graphics used to showcase the product, as well as the overall design and layout of the product page. A well-presented product page can make a significant difference in capturing the attention of potential customers.

In addition to assessing the individual product listings, it is important to consider the overall coherence and consistency of the catalogue as a whole. Look for any discrepancies or contradictions between different sections or categories, and evaluate how well the catalogue as a whole conveys a cohesive and unified brand identity.

When reviewing a product catalogue, it is also important to consider how well it meets the needs and expectations of its target audience. This involves assessing whether the products offered are relevant and appealing to the intended customer base, as well as evaluating how effectively the catalogue communicates the value and benefits of the products.

In addition to evaluating the content and presentation of the catalogue, it is also important to consider its usability and functionality. This includes assessing how easy it is to navigate through the catalogue, search for specific products, and access additional information or resources. A user-friendly and intuitive catalogue can greatly enhance the overall customer experience.

In summary, reviewing a product catalogue involves carefully assessing its content, presentation, coherence, relevance to the target audience, usability, and overall effectiveness. By approaching this task with a systematic and thorough method, you can provide valuable insights and recommendations that can help enhance the quality and impact of the catalogue.

Explore the product catalogues of various POD providers to see what types of items they offer for customization and printing. This can include apparel, accessories, home decor, stationery, and more.

Finally, when reviewing a product catalogue, it is important to provide constructive feedback and suggestions for improvement. This may involve identifying areas where the catalogue could be enhanced or expanded, as well as offering insights into how it could better meet the needs and preferences of its target audience.

Quality and Printing Options: When determining the quality and printing options of print-on-demand services, there are several factors to consider. First and foremost, it is important to assess the overall print quality of the service. This includes evaluating the sharpness and clarity of the text and images, as well as the colour accuracy and consistency. It is also crucial to examine the type of paper and binding options available, as these can significantly impact the overall look and feel of the final product.

In addition to print quality, it is essential to consider the range of printing options offered by the service. This includes assessing the available formats (such as paperback, hardcover, or spiral-bound), as well as any additional features like glossy or matte finishes, embossing, or foil stamping. The ability to customize the printing options according to specific preferences and requirements is also an important consideration.

Another key factor to take into account is the level of customer support and assistance provided by the print-on-demand service. This includes evaluating the ease of the ordering process, as well as the responsiveness and helpfulness of customer service representatives. The availability of online design tools and templates can also be a valuable feature for those looking to self-publish or create custom print materials.

Furthermore, it is important to assess the pricing and cost structure of the print-on-demand service. This includes evaluating the base printing costs, as well as any additional fees for customization, shipping, or expedited production. It is also important to consider any potential discounts or bulk pricing options that may be available for larger orders.

Lastly, it is beneficial to seek out reviews and testimonials from other users of the print-on-demand service in order to gain insight into their experiences and satisfaction with the quality and printing options. This can provide valuable firsthand information about the reliability and consistency of the service, as well as any potential drawbacks or limitations to be aware of.

In conclusion, when determining the quality and printing options of print-on-demand services, it is important to thoroughly evaluate the print quality, range of printing options, customer support, pricing, and user feedback. By carefully considering these factors, individuals and businesses can make informed decisions about which print-on-demand service best meets their specific needs and requirements.

Assess the quality of printing and customization options offered by each provider. Look for details about printing methods, available colours, material options, and customization capabilities.

Pricing and Profit Margins: Understand the pricing structure and profit margins offered by each provider. Compare base costs, shipping rates, and any additional fees to determine how they impact your potential earnings.

Integration with E-Commerce Platforms: Integrating print-on-demand services with an e-commerce platform can be a seamless process with the right approach. To begin with, it's important to choose a print-on-demand provider that offers integration with popular e-commerce platforms such as Shopify, WooCommerce, Etsy, or Amazon. Once the provider is selected, the first step is to create an account and set up the integration with the e-commerce platform. This typically involves installing a plugin or app that allows for seamless communication between the two systems.

After the initial setup is complete, the next step is to upload product designs to the print-on-demand provider's platform. This can include uploading artwork for t-shirts, posters, mugs, or any other customizable products that will be offered for sale on the e-commerce platform. It's important to ensure that the designs meet the provider's specifications for file format, resolution, and colour mode to ensure high-quality printing results.

Once the designs are uploaded, they can be linked to products on the e-commerce platform. This typically involves creating product listings and linking them to the corresponding designs on the print-on-demand provider's platform. It's important to provide accurate and detailed product descriptions, including information about the printing process, materials used, and expected delivery times to set clear expectations for customers.

With the products linked and listings created, it's important to test the integration to ensure that orders flow seamlessly from the e-commerce platform to the print-on-demand provider. This involves placing test orders and verifying that the correct designs are printed and fulfilled according to the specified production and shipping times. It's also important to test the communication between the two systems to ensure that inventory levels are accurately updated and that order status updates are communicated back to the e-commerce platform.

Once the integration is tested and verified, it's important to monitor and manage orders as they come in. This includes reviewing incoming orders, ensuring that designs are correctly applied to each product, and monitoring production and shipping times to ensure that orders are fulfilled in a timely manner. It's also important to provide excellent customer service, including promptly addressing any issues or concerns that may arise with orders placed through the e-commerce platform.

In addition to managing orders, it's important to regularly review and update product listings on the e-commerce platform. This can include adding new designs, updating existing ones, and adjusting pricing or product descriptions as needed. It's also important to monitor sales and customer feedback to identify trends and opportunities for new products or design variations.

Finally, it's important to continuously optimize the integration between the print-on-demand provider and the e-commerce platform. This can include exploring additional features offered by the provider, such as automated order processing or advanced customization options. It's also important to stay informed about updates and changes to both the e-commerce platform and the print-on-demand provider to ensure that the integration remains seamless and up-to-date.

In conclusion, integrating print-on-demand services with an e-commerce platform requires careful planning, attention to detail, and ongoing management. By selecting the right provider, setting up a seamless integration, managing orders effectively, and continuously optimizing the process, businesses can successfully offer customizable products for sale online while minimizing logistical challenges.

Sample Orders: To get sample orders from print-on-demand providers, you first need to choose a print-on-demand company that offers sample orders. Look for companies that allow you to order samples of your own products at a discounted rate. Once you have selected a print-on-demand provider, you will need to sign up for an account and set up your store or products on their platform.

After setting up your products, you can then proceed to order samples. Most print-on-demand providers have a specific process for ordering samples. This may involve navigating to the product you want to order a sample of, selecting the option for sample orders, and then proceeding to checkout. Some companies may offer a discount on sample orders, while others may require you to pay the full price.

It's important to note that the process for ordering samples may vary depending on the print-on-demand provider you choose. Some companies may have specific requirements or restrictions for sample orders, so be sure to carefully review their guidelines before placing an order.

Once you have placed your sample order, you will typically receive an estimated delivery date for your samples. It's important to keep in mind that shipping times may vary depending on your location and the print-on-demand provider's production and shipping processes.

After receiving your samples, take the time to thoroughly inspect the quality of the products. Pay attention to the printing, material, and overall craftsmanship of the items. This will allow you to ensure that the products meet your expectations and standards before offering them to your customers.

If you are satisfied with the quality of the samples, you can then proceed to use the print-on-demand provider to fulfil customer orders. However, if you have any concerns or issues with the samples, be sure to communicate with the print-on-demand company to address any potential issues or make any necessary adjustments to your products.

Getting sample orders from print-on-demand providers involves choosing a company that offers sample orders, setting up your products on their platform, and following their specific process for ordering samples. By carefully reviewing the guidelines and inspecting the quality of the samples, you can ensure that the products meet your standards and are ready to be offered to your customers.

Shipping and Fulfilment: Evaluate the shipping and fulfilment process of each provider. Look for details about shipping times, packaging, tracking information, and customer support for order-related inquiries.

Customer Reviews and Testimonials: When using print-on-demand providers, it is essential to leverage customers' reviews and testimonies to make informed decisions and maximize the potential of your business. First and foremost, it is crucial to thoroughly research and analyze the reviews and testimonies of previous customers. Look for patterns in the feedback, paying attention to aspects such as print quality, shipping times, customer service, and overall satisfaction. This will provide valuable insights into the provider's performance and help you gauge their reliability and quality.

Furthermore, consider the specific needs and preferences of your target audience when evaluating customer reviews. Look for reviews from customers who are similar to your target market in terms of demographics, interests, and purchasing behaviour. This will give you a better understanding of how the provider's services align with the expectations of your potential customers.

In addition to analyzing reviews, it is also beneficial to seek out testimonies from other businesses or individuals within your industry who have used the print-on-demand provider. Their experiences can offer valuable insights into how the provider caters to specific niche markets and whether they are capable of meeting the unique requirements of your business.

Once you have gathered and analyzed a range of customer reviews and testimonies, it is important to use this information to inform your decision-making process. Consider creating a checklist or rating system based on the key criteria identified in the reviews, allowing you to objectively compare different providers and identify the best fit for your business.

Moreover, use the positive aspects highlighted in the reviews and testimonies as a guide for what to look for in a print-on-demand provider. For example, if multiple customers praise a provider for their quick turnaround times, this may be a crucial factor for your business if you prioritize fast order fulfilment.

On the other hand, pay close attention to any recurring negative feedback and consider how these issues may impact your business. If multiple customers express dissatisfaction with the print quality or packaging, this could be a red flag that the provider may not meet your standards for product quality and presentation.

Incorporating customers' reviews and testimonies into your decision-making process can also help you anticipate potential challenges and plan accordingly. For instance, if multiple reviews mention delays in shipping or difficulties with customer support, you can proactively address these issues by setting clear expectations with your customers and having contingency plans in place.

Furthermore, consider reaching out to the print-on-demand providers directly to address any concerns or questions that arise from the customer reviews. Use the feedback from previous customers as a basis for discussing specific areas of improvement or clarification with the provider, allowing you to make an informed decision based on their responses.

Ultimately, leveraging customers' reviews and testimonies when choosing a print-on-demand provider can significantly mitigate risks and increase the likelihood of a successful partnership; this is achieved carefully considering the experiences of others, you can make informed decisions that align with the needs of your business and your target audience, ultimately leading to a more seamless and successful print-on-demand experience.

Terms of Service and Policies: When reviewing the terms and conditions of services for print-on-demand services, there are several key aspects to consider. First and foremost, it is important to carefully read through the entire document to ensure a comprehensive understanding of the terms and conditions. This includes paying attention to any specific requirements or restrictions that may apply to the use of the print-on-demand services, such as limitations on the types of content that can be printed or sold.

It is also important to review the pricing and payment terms outlined in the terms and conditions. This includes understanding the fees associated with using the print-on-demand services, as well as any potential additional costs that may apply. It is important to be aware of any minimum sales requirements or other financial obligations that may be imposed by the service provider.

Another important aspect to consider when reviewing the terms and conditions of print-on-demand services is the intellectual property rights and licensing terms. This includes understanding who retains ownership of the content that is uploaded to the print-on-demand platform, as well as any licensing agreements that may be in place. It is important to ensure that the terms and conditions align with your own intellectual property rights and that you are comfortable with the licensing arrangements outlined in the document.

In addition, it is important to review the terms and conditions related to fulfilment and shipping. This includes understanding the process for fulfilling orders, as well as any shipping options that may be available. It is important to be aware of any potential limitations or restrictions that may apply to the fulfilment and shipping process, as well as any associated costs.

Furthermore, it is important to carefully review the terms and conditions related to customer service and support. This includes understanding the process for handling customer inquiries and issues, as well as any potential service level agreements that may be in place. It is important to ensure that the customer service and support terms align with your own expectations and requirements for providing a positive customer experience.

Lastly, it is important to review the terms and conditions related to termination and suspension of services. This includes understanding the circumstances under which the service provider may terminate or suspend your access to the print-on-demand services, as well as any potential implications for your business. It is important to be aware of any potential risks or liabilities associated with termination or suspension, as well as any potential recourse that may be available.

please note that reviewing the terms and conditions of services for print-on-demand services requires careful attention to detail and a comprehensive understanding of the various aspects outlined in the document. By carefully reviewing and considering each of these key aspects, you can ensure that you are fully informed and prepared to make an informed decision about using print-on-demand services for your business.

Steps to Explore the Advantages of Print on Demand Services:

By thoroughly exploring print-on-demand services using these steps, you can make informed decisions about which provider best aligns with your business goals,

Choose a Niche: Select a niche or market segment for your print-on-demand products. Consider popular themes, hobbies, or specific interests that have a dedicated audience.

Research Print-on-Demand Platforms: Explore print-on-demand platforms such as Printful, Printify, and Teespring. Compare their product offerings, printing quality, shipping options, and integration capabilities with e-commerce platforms.

Design Custom Products: Create or commission unique designs for your print-on-demand products, such as T-shirts, mugs, phone cases, and more. Ensure that your designs are original or properly licensed.

Set Up an Online Store: Create an online store using e-commerce platforms like Shopify, Etsy, or WooCommerce. Customize your store to reflect your brand and showcase your print-on-demand products.

Integrate with Print-on-Demand Services: Integrate your online store with the selected print-on-demand platform to enable seamless order fulfilment and printing of custom products.

Marketing and Promotion: Develop a marketing strategy to drive traffic to your store and promote your print-on-demand products. Utilize social media, influencer partnerships, content marketing, and email marketing to reach potential customers.

Customer Service: Provide excellent customer service to build trust and loyalty. Be responsive to customer inquiries and ensure timely order fulfilment.

Analyze Sales Data: Regularly analyze sales data and customer feedback to understand which products are performing well and which designs resonate with your audience.

Expand Product Line: Consider expanding your product offerings based on customer demand and market trends. Explore new product categories and experiment with different designs.

Scale Your Business: As your business grows, optimize your operations, explore new marketing channels, and consider offering personalized or custom design services.

By following these steps, you can start making money by exploring print-on-demand services. If you have any specific questions or need further guidance, feel free to ask!

Chapter 5
Generating Income Through Affiliate Marketing.

Affiliate marketing another source of making money online.

Affiliate marketing is a type of performance-based marketing in which a business rewards one or more affiliates for each visitor or customer brought by the affiliate's own marketing efforts. The affiliate earns a commission for generating sales, leads, or traffic to the merchant's website through their promotional activities. This form of marketing is beneficial for both the merchant and the affiliate, as it allows the merchant to reach a larger audience and increase sales, while the affiliate can earn passive income by promoting products or services they believe in.

Affiliate marketing operates on a revenue-sharing model, where the affiliate receives a portion of the revenue generated from the sale of the merchant's products or services. This commission can be based on a percentage of the sale price, a fixed amount per sale, or a combination of both. The affiliate's role is to drive traffic to the merchant's website through various marketing channels such as content marketing, social media, email marketing, search engine optimization, and paid advertising. The success of affiliate marketing relies on the ability of the affiliate to effectively promote the merchant's products or services to their audience.

Affiliate marketing originated in the late 1980s, around the time when the internet was just beginning to gain popularity. It was a concept that emerged as a way for companies to reach a larger audience through the use of independent individuals or companies to promote their products or services. This form of marketing allowed businesses to leverage the reach and influence of these affiliates, who would then earn a commission for every sale or lead they generated. The idea behind affiliate marketing was to create a win-win situation where both the company and the affiliate would benefit from the partnership.

The concept of affiliate marketing gained traction as more and more companies began to recognize the potential of leveraging the power of the internet and its ability to connect people on a global scale. With the rise of e-commerce and online shopping, affiliate marketing became an attractive option for businesses looking to expand their reach and increase their sales. This led to the development of various affiliate marketing programs and networks, which provided a platform for companies to connect with potential affiliates and manage their partnerships more effectively.

As the internet continued to evolve, so did affiliate marketing. New technologies and platforms emerged, offering more sophisticated tracking and reporting capabilities, as well as better ways to manage and optimize affiliate partnerships. This allowed businesses to gain deeper insights into their affiliate marketing efforts and make more informed decisions about their partnerships. Additionally, the rise of social media and influencer marketing further fueled the growth of affiliate marketing, as individuals with large followings began to partner with brands to promote their products and services.

Today, affiliate marketing has become a multi-billion dollar industry, with businesses of all sizes leveraging the power of affiliate partnerships to drive sales and grow their customer base. The landscape of affiliate marketing has also become more diverse, with affiliates ranging from individual bloggers and social media influencers to large media companies and online publishers. As technology continues to advance, affiliate marketing is expected to evolve even further, providing new opportunities for businesses and affiliates alike to collaborate and achieve mutual success in the digital age.

Affiliate marketing is an attractive option for individuals looking to monetize their online presence, as it offers a low barrier to entry and the potential for high earnings. It allows individuals to leverage their existing audience or create new channels for promoting products and earning commissions. Additionally, affiliate marketing provides flexibility in terms of working hours and location, making it an appealing option for those seeking a remote or flexible work arrangement. With the rise of e-commerce and digital marketing, affiliate marketing has become an increasingly popular way for individuals to generate income online.

One of the key benefits of affiliate marketing is its cost-effectiveness for merchants, as they only pay for performance. This means that they do not incur upfront costs for advertising or marketing efforts, and only pay when a desired action is completed, such as a sale or lead generation. Additionally, affiliate marketing allows merchants to tap into new markets and reach potential customers that they may not have been able to reach through traditional advertising methods. This can lead to increased brand exposure and sales, ultimately benefiting both the merchant and the affiliate.

Affiliate marketing also offers benefits for consumers, as it provides them with access to a wide range of products and services through various online channels. Affiliates often provide valuable content and recommendations to their audience, helping consumers make informed purchasing decisions. This can result in a more personalized shopping experience for consumers, as they are exposed to products and services that align with their interests and preferences. Additionally, consumers may benefit from special promotions or discounts offered by affiliates, further enhancing their shopping experience.

To summarize the above said, affiliate marketing is a performance-based marketing strategy that benefits merchants, affiliates, and consumers alike. It offers a cost-effective way for merchants to reach new customers and increase sales, while providing affiliates with an opportunity to earn passive income by promoting products they believe in. Consumers benefit from access to a wide range of products and services through various online channels, along with valuable content and recommendations from affiliates. With its low barrier to entry and potential for high earnings, affiliate marketing has become a popular option for individuals looking to monetize their online presence and generate income through digital marketing efforts.

Generating income through affiliate marketing involves promoting products or services offered by other companies and earning a commission for each sale or action generated through your promotional efforts. Here's an overview of how affiliate marketing works and how individuals can generate income through this model:

Affiliate marketing offers individuals the opportunity to earn income by leveraging their digital presence and promotional skills to drive sales and actions for other businesses. Successful affiliates often build niche-specific content, establish authority in their chosen industry, and develop relationships with their audience to effectively promote products and services.

The main reason why people do affiliate marketing:

Affiliate marketing has become a popular choice for many people due to its potential for generating passive income. One of the main reasons why individuals are drawn to affiliate marketing is the opportunity to earn money without having to create their own products or services. Instead, affiliate marketers can promote and sell other people's products and earn a commission for each sale they make. This means that individuals can start an affiliate marketing business with minimal investment and potentially earn a significant income over time.

Another reason why people are attracted to affiliate marketing is the flexibility it offers. Unlike traditional 9-5 jobs, affiliate marketers have the freedom to work from anywhere with an internet connection. This means that they can create their own schedule and work at their own pace, making it an appealing option for those who value flexibility and freedom in their work.

Additionally, affiliate marketing allows individuals to tap into a global market. With the rise of e-commerce, there are countless products and services available online, and affiliate marketers can promote these offerings to a worldwide audience. This opens up a vast potential for earning income and provides the opportunity to reach customers from diverse backgrounds and cultures.

Moreover, affiliate marketing provides an opportunity for individuals to leverage their existing online presence. Many bloggers, social media influencers, and content creators already have a following, and affiliate marketing allows them to monetize their platforms by promoting products and services that align with their audience's interests. This can be a lucrative way for individuals to turn their passion or hobby into a source of income.

Furthermore, affiliate marketing offers a low barrier to entry, making it accessible to people from all walks of life. Whether someone is a stay-at-home parent, a student, or a full-time employee looking to diversify their income streams, affiliate marketing can be a viable option. With the right strategies and dedication, individuals can build a successful affiliate marketing business without needing specialized skills or experience.

In addition, the potential for passive income is a major draw for many people considering affiliate marketing. Once an affiliate marketer has set up their promotional channels and established a steady flow of traffic, they can continue to earn commissions from sales without having to actively work on each transaction. This means that affiliate marketers can potentially earn money while they sleep or focus on other aspects of their lives.

Moreover, affiliate marketing allows individuals to learn valuable skills in digital marketing and sales. As they work on promoting products and optimizing their strategies, affiliate marketers can gain insights into consumer behaviour, effective marketing techniques, and sales tactics. These skills can be transferable to other areas of business and can be valuable for personal and professional development.

Additionally, the low overhead costs associated with affiliate marketing make it an attractive option for those looking to start a business without significant financial risk. Unlike traditional businesses that require inventory, storefronts, or employees, affiliate marketing can be started with minimal investment in website hosting, marketing tools, and advertising. This makes it a low-cost way for individuals to dip their toes into entrepreneurship and potentially scale their business over time.

Finally, the potential for scalability is another reason why people are drawn to affiliate marketing. As an individual gains experience and builds their online presence, they can expand their reach and increase their earnings by promoting multiple products across various niches. This scalability allows affiliate marketers to grow their income streams and achieve financial freedom over time.

Methods of Generating Income through Affiliate Marketing are as follows:

Affiliate marketing is a popular method of generating income by promoting products or services and earning a commission for each sale or lead that is generated through your unique affiliate link. One of the key advantages of affiliate marketing is that it allows individuals to earn money without having to create their own products or services. Instead, affiliates can focus on promoting existing products and earning a commission for the sales they generate.

To get started with affiliate marketing, the first step is to find a niche or industry that you are passionate about and that has a demand for products or services. Once you have identified your niche, the next step is to research and identify potential affiliate programs that offer products or services relevant to your niche. This can be done through affiliate networks, which are platforms that connect affiliates with merchants offering affiliate programs.

After finding suitable affiliate programs, the next step is to create content that promotes the products or services you are affiliated with. This can include writing blog posts, creating videos, or sharing content on social media platforms. The key is to create high-quality, engaging content that provides value to your audience and encourages them to click on your affiliate links and make a purchase.

In addition to creating content, it is important to focus on building and growing your audience. This can be done through various marketing strategies such as search engine optimization (SEO), social media marketing, email marketing, and paid advertising. By growing your audience and building trust with them, you can increase the likelihood of them clicking on your affiliate links and making a purchase.

Another important aspect of affiliate marketing is tracking and analyzing your results. This involves monitoring the performance of your affiliate links, tracking the number of clicks and sales generated, and analyzing the effectiveness of your marketing efforts. By understanding which strategies that are working and which are not, you can optimize your approach and improve your results over time.

One of the key benefits of affiliate marketing is that it offers a flexible and scalable income opportunity. As you continue to grow your audience and refine your marketing strategies, you have the potential to increase your earnings significantly. Additionally, because affiliate marketing can be done from anywhere with an internet connection, it offers the flexibility to work from home or while travelling.

In summary, affiliate marketing is a method of generating income by promoting products or services and earning a commission for each sale or lead that is generated through your unique affiliate link. By identifying a niche, finding suitable affiliate programs, creating high-quality content, building and growing an audience, and tracking and analyzing results, individuals can build a successful affiliate marketing business. With its flexibility and scalability, affiliate marketing offers a lucrative income opportunity for those willing to put in the time and effort to succeed. The following steps are very necessary.

Choose Your Niche:

A niche in affiliate marketing refers to a specific segment of the market that a marketer targets with their promotional efforts. This segment is characterized by its unique needs, preferences, and interests, and it represents a distinct subset of the larger market. Identifying a niche is crucial for affiliate marketers as it allows them to focus their resources on a particular group of potential customers who are more likely to be interested in the products or services being promoted.

In affiliate marketing, a niche can be defined based on various factors such as demographics, interests, hobbies, or problems that a particular group of people may have. For example, a niche could be "stay-at-home moms looking for ways to make extra income" or "fitness enthusiasts seeking high-protein meal recipes." By narrowing down their target audience to a specific niche, affiliate marketers can tailor their marketing strategies and content to better resonate with the needs and desires of that particular group.

Choosing the right niche is essential for affiliate marketers to maximize their chances of success. A well-defined niche allows marketers to position themselves as experts in a specific area and build credibility and trust with their audience. It also enables them to create content that is highly relevant and valuable to their target market, increasing the likelihood of driving engagement and conversions.

Moreover, targeting a niche can help affiliate marketers stand out in a crowded marketplace. Instead of competing with countless other marketers for the attention of a broad audience, focusing on a niche allows them to differentiate themselves and offer specialized solutions to a specific set of problems or desires. This can lead to higher conversion rates and more loyal customers who appreciate the personalized approach.

In addition, niche marketing can be more cost-effective and efficient for affiliate marketers. By concentrating their efforts on a well-defined niche, they can allocate their resources more strategically, whether it's through paid advertising, content creation, or relationship building. This targeted approach can result in higher returns on investment and lower acquisition costs compared to trying to appeal to a broad and diverse audience.

Furthermore, a niche can provide long-term sustainability for affiliate marketers. Building a brand and a following within a specific niche can lead to ongoing opportunities for monetization and growth. As the marketer becomes established as an authority within their niche, they can expand their offerings, form partnerships with relevant brands, and continue to serve the evolving needs of their audience.

Ultimately, finding the right niche is a balance between market demand and personal passion or expertise. While it's important to choose a niche with sufficient potential for profitability and growth, it's also beneficial for affiliate marketers to select a niche that aligns with their own interests or knowledge. This can make the marketing efforts more enjoyable and authentic, leading to better engagement and rapport with the target audience.

In conclusion, a niche in affiliate marketing represents a specialized segment of the market that affiliate marketers target with their promotional activities. By identifying and focusing on a specific niche, marketers can tailor their strategies, build credibility, differentiate themselves, and achieve cost-effective results. Choosing the right niche is essential for long-term success in affiliate marketing and requires a balance of market potential and personal alignment.

When choosing a niche for your affiliate marketing business, it's important to consider several factors to ensure you select a profitable and sustainable niche. First, consider your own interests and passions. Choosing a niche that aligns with your interests will not only make the work more enjoyable, but it will also allow you to leverage your existing knowledge and expertise in the area. This can give you a competitive edge and help you create valuable content that resonates with your audience.

Next, consider the profitability and demand of the niche. Look for niches that have a large and engaged audience, as well as a proven track record of purchasing products or services. Research the competition within the niche to ensure there is room for you to carve out a unique position and attract your own audience. Additionally, consider the potential for recurring revenue within the niche, such as subscription-based products or services, which can provide long-term income opportunities.

It's also important to consider the level of competition within the niche. While some competition is a good sign that there is demand for products or services, too much competition can make it difficult to stand out and attract customers. Look for niches where you can differentiate yourself and offer something unique to your audience. This could be through specialized knowledge, unique products, or a distinct brand identity.

Furthermore, consider the affiliate programs available within the niche. Look for programs that offer competitive commission rates, high-quality products or services, and reliable tracking and payment systems. It's also important to consider the reputation of the companies behind the affiliate programs, as you want to ensure you are partnering with reputable and trustworthy businesses.

Another important factor to consider is the potential for growth within the niche. Look for niches that are evolving and expanding, rather than ones that are stagnant or declining. This could include emerging trends, new technologies, or changing consumer behaviors that present opportunities for innovation and growth within the niche.

Lastly, consider the long-term sustainability of the niche. Avoid niches that are based on fads or short-lived trends, as these can quickly become outdated and leave you with a dwindling audience. Instead, look for niches with enduring appeal and ongoing demand, ensuring that your affiliate marketing business has the potential for long-term success.

It is important to note that, when choosing a niche for your affiliate marketing business, consider your own interests, the profitability and demand of the niche, the level of competition, the available affiliate programs, the potential for growth, and the long-term sustainability of the niche. By carefully evaluating these factors, you can select a niche that aligns with your strengths and goals, while also offering ample opportunities for success in the competitive world of affiliate marketing.

Selecting a bad niche can affect the overall performance of your affiliate marketing. Bad niche in affiliate marketing can have several disadvantages. Firstly, it can lead to low demand for the products or services being promoted, resulting in lower sales and commissions. This can be frustrating for affiliate marketers who put in time and effort to promote products that simply don't resonate with their audience. Additionally, a bad niche can also mean facing stiff competition from other affiliates, making it harder to stand out and make an impact in the market.

Moreover, a bad niche may not offer enough opportunities for creating valuable content or engaging with a target audience. This can limit the potential for building a loyal following and establishing credibility as an authority in the niche. Without a strong connection to the niche, affiliate marketers may struggle to create compelling marketing campaigns that drive conversions and generate income.

Furthermore, a bad niche can also lead to difficulties in finding suitable affiliate programs with attractive commission structures. Some niches may have limited options for affiliate partnerships or may offer lower commission rates, making it harder for marketers to earn significant income from their efforts. This can be discouraging and may lead to a lack of motivation to continue pursuing affiliate marketing in that particular niche.

Selecting a bad niche can result in a mismatch between the marketer's interests and the products or services being promoted. This can make it challenging to maintain enthusiasm and passion for the work, leading to burnout and a lack of long-term sustainability in the affiliate marketing business. Without genuine interest in the niche, it can be difficult to stay motivated and consistently produce high-quality content and marketing strategies.

Choosing a bad niche in affiliate marketing can have several drawbacks, including low demand for products, intense competition, limited opportunities for content creation, and challenges in finding suitable affiliate programs, and a potential mismatch with the marketer's interests. It's crucial for affiliate marketers to carefully research and select a niche that aligns with market demand, offers opportunities for growth, and resonates with their own passions and expertise.

Research Affiliate Programs:

Affiliate programs are a type of performance-based marketing in which a business rewards one or more affiliates for each visitor or customer brought by the affiliate's own marketing efforts. This means that affiliates are essentially salespeople who promote a company's products or services and earn a commission for every sale or lead they generate. The concept is simple: affiliates promote a product or service through various marketing channels, such as websites, social media, email, or other online platforms, and earn a commission for every sale or lead they drive to the company's website.

Affiliate programs are popular among businesses because they offer a cost-effective way to market their products or services. Instead of spending money on traditional advertising and marketing campaigns, businesses can leverage the power of affiliate marketing to reach a wider audience and drive more sales. For affiliates, these programs offer an opportunity to earn passive income by promoting products or services that they believe in and are passionate about. It's a win-win situation for both parties involved.

The key to a successful affiliate program is building strong relationships with affiliates and providing them with the tools and support they need to be successful. This includes offering competitive commission rates, providing access to marketing materials and resources, and offering regular communication and support. By nurturing these relationships, businesses can create a network of loyal affiliates who are motivated to promote their products or services and drive sales.

Affiliate programs come in various forms, including pay-per-sale, pay-per-lead, and pay-per-click models. In a pay-per-sale model, affiliates earn a commission for every sale they generate, while in a pay-per-lead model, they earn a commission for every lead they generate. In a pay-per-click model, affiliates earn a commission for every click they drive to the company's website. Each model has its own advantages and disadvantages, and businesses can choose the one that best fits their goals and objectives.

One of the key benefits of affiliate programs is the ability to reach a wider audience and drive more sales. Affiliates have their own unique audience and marketing channels, which can help businesses, reach potential customers that they may not have been able to reach through traditional marketing efforts. This can result in increased brand awareness, higher website traffic, and ultimately more sales.

Another benefit of affiliate programs is the ability to track and measure the performance of marketing efforts. Businesses can use tracking tools and analytics to monitor the success of their affiliate marketing campaigns, including the number of clicks, leads, and sales generated by each affiliate. This data can help businesses make informed decisions about their marketing strategies and optimize their affiliate programs for better results.

In conclusion, affiliate programs are a powerful marketing tool that can help businesses reach a wider audience, drive more sales, and increase brand awareness. For affiliates, these programs offer an opportunity to earn passive income by promoting products or services that they believe in. By building strong relationships with affiliates and providing them with the tools and support they need to be successful, businesses can create a network of loyal affiliates who are motivated to promote their products or services and drive sales.

When researching for a good affiliate program, it's important to start by defining your niche and target audience. Understanding who you want to reach and what products or services would appeal to them is crucial in finding the right affiliate program. Once you have a clear understanding of your niche, you can start researching different affiliate programs that align with your audience's interests.

One of the first things to consider when researching affiliate programs is the commission structure. Look for programs that offer competitive commission rates and a clear outline of how you will earn money through referrals. It's also important to consider the cookie duration, which is the length of time that a referral will be tracked back to your affiliate link. Ideally, you want a program with long cookie duration to maximize your earning potential.

Another important factor to consider is the quality of the products or services offered by the affiliate program. Research the company's reputation, customer reviews, and product quality to ensure that you are promoting something that you can stand behind. It's also important to consider the level of support and resources provided to affiliates, such as marketing materials, tracking tools, and dedicated support staff.

When researching affiliate programs, it's essential to consider the payment methods and schedule. Look for programs that offer reliable and convenient payment options, such as direct deposit, PayPal, or wire transfer. Additionally, make sure to review the program's payment schedule to ensure that you will receive timely payouts for your referrals.

It's also important to research the affiliate program's terms and conditions to fully understand the rules and requirements for participation. Look for programs with transparent and fair terms that align with your business practices and goals. Pay attention to any restrictions on promotional methods, as well as any exclusivity clauses that may limit your ability to promote competing products or services.

In addition to these factors, it's important to research the affiliate program's track record and performance. Look for programs with a proven track record of success, including a history of timely payments, strong conversion rates, and a positive reputation within the industry. Researching the program's performance can help you make an informed decision about whether it's a good fit for your business.

When researching for a good affiliate program, it's also important to consider the level of competition within your niche. Look for programs that offer unique products or services that are not oversaturated in the market. Consider the level of competition you will face when promoting the program and whether there is room for growth and success.

Finally, it's important to research the affiliate program's marketing and promotional materials. Look for programs that provide affiliates with a range of marketing materials, such as banners, text links, and email templates, to help you effectively promote their products or services. Additionally, consider whether the program offers any training or resources to help you maximize your earning potential and succeed as an affiliate marketer.

In conclusion, researching for a good affiliate program involves considering a range of factors, including commission structure, product quality, support and resources, payment methods, terms and conditions, track record and performance, competition, and marketing materials. By thoroughly researching these factors, you can make an informed decision about which affiliate programs are the best fit for your business and audience.

Ensure that you identify reputable affiliate programs within your chosen niche. Look for programs offered by well-known brands, e-commerce platforms, and digital products/services providers such as, Clickbank, Digistore24 etc. Affiliate networks such as ClickBank and Digistore24 are excellent platforms for affiliate programs. These networks provide a wide range of products and services that affiliates can promote, allowing them to earn commissions on sales. ClickBank, for example, offers a diverse selection of digital products, including e-books, software, and online courses, making it a great choice for affiliates looking to promote digital goods. Similarly, Digistore24 specializes in digital products and offers a user-friendly platform for affiliates to find and promote products.

One of the key benefits of affiliate networks like ClickBank and Digistore24 is the variety of products available for promotion. Affiliates can choose from thousands of products in various niches, allowing them to find products that align with their interests and target audience. Additionally, these networks often provide detailed statistics and analytics, allowing affiliates to track their performance and optimize their promotional efforts.

Furthermore, affiliate networks typically offer competitive commission rates, making it possible for affiliates to earn significant income through their promotional efforts. ClickBank, for example, allows affiliates to earn commissions ranging from 50% to 75% on product sales, providing a lucrative opportunity for those who are successful in driving sales. Similarly, Digistore24 offers generous commission rates on digital products, making it an attractive option for affiliates seeking high earning potential.

In addition to the wide selection of products and competitive commission rates, affiliate networks often provide resources and support for affiliates to succeed. This may include marketing materials, training resources, and dedicated affiliate managers who can offer guidance and assistance. By leveraging these resources, affiliates can enhance their promotional strategies and increase their earning potential.

Moreover, affiliate networks like ClickBank and Digistore24 offer reliable tracking and payment systems, ensuring that affiliates receive accurate credit for their referrals and timely payments for their commissions. This level of transparency and reliability is essential for building trust between affiliates and product vendors, ultimately contributing to the success of the affiliate programs.

Another advantage of affiliate networks is the opportunity for affiliates to build relationships with product vendors and other affiliates within the network. This can lead to collaboration opportunities, joint ventures, and access to exclusive promotional materials or offers, further enhancing the earning potential for affiliates.

Overall, affiliate networks such as ClickBank and Digistore24 offer a wealth of opportunities for affiliates to promote products and earn commissions. With their diverse product offerings, competitive commission rates, resources and support, reliable tracking and payment systems, and potential for collaboration, these networks are well-suited for individuals looking to succeed in affiliate marketing. Whether you are a seasoned affiliate marketer or just starting out, these networks provide a solid foundation for building a successful affiliate business.

Join Affiliate Networks:

An affiliate network is a platform that connects advertisers with publishers who are willing to promote their products or services. Advertisers join the network to gain access to a wide range of publishers who can help them reach their target audience and increase their sales. Publishers, on the other hand, join the network to find relevant offers to promote on their websites, blogs, or social media channels.

Affiliate networks provide a centralized platform for advertisers to manage their affiliate programs and for publishers to find and promote offers. They offer a range of tools and resources to help both advertisers and publishers track performance, manage payments, and optimize their campaigns. This includes tracking links, reporting dashboards, and payment processing systems.

One of the key benefits of an affiliate network is that it allows advertisers to reach a wider audience without having to invest in additional marketing efforts. By leveraging the network's existing relationships with publishers, advertisers can quickly scale their affiliate programs and reach new customers. Similarly, publishers can access a wide range of offers from different advertisers, allowing them to monetize their traffic more effectively.

Affiliate networks also play a crucial role in ensuring that both advertisers and publishers adhere to best practices and industry standards. They often provide guidelines and policies to help maintain the quality of offers and traffic within the network. Additionally, they may offer support and resources to help advertisers and publishers maximize their success within the network.

In addition to connecting advertisers with publishers, affiliate networks also act as intermediaries in the payment process. They handle the tracking of sales and commissions, as well as the distribution of payments to publishers. This helps streamline the payment process for both advertisers and publishers, ensuring that commissions are accurately tracked and paid out in a timely manner.

An affiliate network serves as a valuable ecosystem for advertisers and publishers to connect, collaborate, and grow their businesses. It provides a platform for advertisers to expand their reach and increase sales, while offering publishers opportunities to monetize their traffic and promote relevant offers to their audience. Through the network's tools, resources, and support, both advertisers and publishers can effectively manage their affiliate marketing efforts and achieve mutual success.

Good affiliate networks are crucial for both advertisers and publishers. They provide a platform for advertisers to reach a wider audience and for publishers to monetize their traffic effectively. A good affiliate network offers a wide range of high-quality offers from reputable advertisers, ensuring that publishers have access to the best opportunities to generate revenue. Additionally, they provide robust tracking and reporting tools, allowing both advertisers and publishers to monitor and optimize their campaigns for maximum effectiveness.

Furthermore, good affiliate networks offer excellent support and guidance to their partners. They provide resources and training to help publishers optimize their traffic and maximize their earnings. For advertisers, they offer assistance in creating and optimizing their offers to attract the right audience and generate the best results. This support is crucial for both parties to succeed in the affiliate marketing space.

In addition, good affiliate networks prioritize transparency and trust. They provide clear terms and conditions, as well as fair and timely payments to their partners. This transparency builds trust and confidence among advertisers and publishers, fostering long-term partnerships and mutual success.

Moreover, good affiliate networks are constantly evolving and adapting to the changing landscape of affiliate marketing. They stay ahead of industry trends and technology advancements, offering innovative solutions to meet the needs of their partners. This adaptability ensures that both advertisers and publishers can stay competitive in the market and continue to grow their businesses.

Another important aspect of good affiliate networks is their commitment to compliance and ethical practices. They adhere to industry regulations and best practices, ensuring that all parties operate within legal and ethical boundaries. This commitment protects the reputation of the network and its partners, while also promoting a healthy and sustainable affiliate marketing ecosystem.

Furthermore, good affiliate networks foster a sense of community among their partners. They provide opportunities for networking and collaboration, allowing publishers and advertisers to connect and share insights and experiences. This sense of community not only enriches the partnership experience but also contributes to the overall growth and success of the network.

Additionally, good affiliate networks offer advanced technology and tools to streamline the affiliate marketing process. They provide user-friendly interfaces, advanced tracking systems, and optimization tools that empower partners to manage their campaigns efficiently and effectively. This technology-driven approach enhances the overall experience for both advertisers and publishers, making it easier for them to achieve their goals.

Moreover, good affiliate networks prioritize quality over quantity. They carefully vet advertisers and offers to ensure that only the best opportunities are available to publishers. This focus on quality leads to higher conversion rates and better results for both advertisers and publishers, ultimately driving success for all parties involved.

In conclusion, good affiliate networks play a crucial role in the success of both advertisers and publishers in the affiliate marketing industry. By offering high-quality offers, robust support, transparency, adaptability, compliance, community, advanced technology, and a focus on quality, they create an environment where all partners can thrive and achieve their business objectives.

Affiliate networks you can join include but not limited to Amazon Associates, ShareASale, CJ Affiliate, and Rakuten Marketing. These networks offer a wide range of affiliate programs across different niches.

Build a Platform:

Create a platform to promote affiliate products, such as a blog, website, YouTube channel, or social media presence. Your platform should provide valuable content related to your niche. To build a platform to generate money through affiliate marketing, the first step is to choose a niche that you are passionate about and that has a good potential for affiliate products. This could be anything from fitness and health to technology or fashion. Once you have chosen your niche, it's important to research and understand your target audience. This will help you tailor your content and promotions to their needs and preferences.

Next, you'll need to set up a website or blog where you can create and share valuable content related to your chosen niche. This could include product reviews, how-to guides, and informative articles. Make sure your website is visually appealing, easy to navigate, and optimized for search engines to attract organic traffic.

After setting up your website, it's time to start building an audience through various channels such as social media, email marketing, and search engine optimization (SEO). Engage with your audience by providing valuable content and building a community around your niche.

Once you have a decent amount of traffic coming to your website, it's time to start promoting affiliate products. Look for reputable affiliate programs that offer products relevant to your niche and align with your audience's interests. Promote these products through your website content, email marketing campaigns, and social media channels.

In addition to promoting affiliate products, consider creating your own digital products or services that complement the affiliate products you are promoting. This could include e-books, online courses, or consulting services. By diversifying your revenue streams, you can maximize your earning potential.

As your platform grows, consider reaching out to other influencers and bloggers in your niche for collaboration opportunities. This could include guest posting, joint promotions, or co-hosting events. Collaborating with others can help you reach a wider audience and build credibility in your niche.

To track your progress and optimize your affiliate marketing strategy, use analytics tools to monitor your website traffic, conversion rates, and sales. This data will help you identify which strategies are working and which ones need improvement.

Always prioritize providing value to your audience. Building trust and credibility with your audience is crucial for long-term success in affiliate marketing. Be transparent about your affiliate partnerships and only promote products that you genuinely believe in and that will benefit your audience.

Building a platform for affiliate marketing requires careful planning, consistent effort, and a focus on providing value to your audience. By choosing the right niche, creating valuable content, promoting relevant affiliate products, and diversifying your revenue streams, you can build a successful platform that generates money through affiliate marketing.

Create Valuable Content:

Creating valuable content for affiliate marketing involves understanding your audience, providing valuable information, and promoting products that align with your audience's needs and interests. To start, it's essential to research your target audience to understand their pain points, interests, and preferences. This will help you create content that resonates with them and provides solutions to their problems. Additionally, conducting keyword research can help you identify popular topics and trends within your niche, allowing you to create content that has the potential to rank well in search engines.

Once you have a clear understanding of your audience and their needs, it's important to create high-quality, valuable content that provides useful information, educates your audience, and solve their problems. This can include blog posts, how-to guides, product reviews, and comparison articles. The key is to offer content that is genuinely helpful and informative, rather than solely focusing on promoting products. By establishing yourself as a trusted source of information within your niche, you can build credibility and trust with your audience, making them more likely to purchase products through your affiliate links.

In addition to creating valuable written content, incorporating visual elements such as images, infographics, and videos can enhance the overall quality of your content and make it more engaging for your audience. Visual content can help illustrate key points, break up text, and provide a more immersive experience for your audience. This can lead to increased engagement with your content and ultimately drive more traffic and conversions through your affiliate links.

Another important aspect of creating valuable content for affiliate marketing is to focus on promoting products that are genuinely beneficial to your audience. It's crucial to only promote products that you believe in and that align with the needs and interests of your audience. By doing so, you can maintain the trust of your audience and avoid damaging your reputation as a credible source of information. When promoting products, be transparent about your affiliate relationships and provide honest reviews and recommendations to help your audience make informed purchasing decisions.

Furthermore, it's essential to optimize your content for search engines to increase its visibility and reach a larger audience. This involves incorporating relevant keywords, optimizing meta tags, and creating high-quality back-links to improve your content's search engine rankings. By making your content more discoverable, you can attract more organic traffic and increase the likelihood of generating affiliate sales.

Additionally, leveraging social media platforms to promote your content can help expand your reach and drive more traffic to your affiliate links. Sharing valuable content on platforms such as Facebook, Instagram, Twitter, and LinkedIn can help you connect with a wider audience and build a community around your niche. Engaging with your followers, participating in relevant discussions, and sharing valuable insights can help establish you as an authority within your niche and drive more traffic and conversions through your affiliate links.

It's also important to continuously analyze the performance of your content to identify areas for improvement and optimize your strategies for generating affiliate sales. This involves tracking key metrics such as traffic, engagement, conversion rates, and revenue generated from affiliate links. By understanding which types of content resonate most with your audience and drive the highest conversions, you can refine your content strategy to maximize its effectiveness.

Furthermore, staying up to date with industry trends, changes in consumer behaviour, and new product releases can help you create timely and relevant content that captures the attention of your audience. By staying informed about the latest developments in your niche, you can position yourself as a valuable source of information and provide insights that are both informative and actionable for your audience.

In conclusion, creating valuable content for affiliate marketing involves understanding your audience, providing high-quality information, promoting relevant products, optimizing for search engines, leveraging social media, analyzing performance, and staying informed about industry trends. By focusing on delivering genuine value to your audience and building trust through valuable content, you can generate money through affiliate marketing while establishing yourself as a credible authority within your niche.

Promote Affiliate Products:

Affiliate products are items or services that are promoted and sold by individuals or companies known as affiliates. These affiliates earn a commission for every sale they generate through their marketing efforts. The products can range from physical goods like clothing, electronics, and home appliances to digital products such as e-books, online courses, and software. Essentially, affiliate products are any offerings that can be promoted and sold through an affiliate marketing program.

Affiliate products are typically provided by companies or businesses that want to expand their reach and increase sales. By enlisting affiliates to promote their products, these companies can tap into new markets and audiences that they may not have been able to reach on their own. This allows for a wider distribution of their products and can result in increased brand awareness and revenue.

Affiliate products are often marketed through various channels including websites, blogs, social media platforms, email marketing, and online advertising. Affiliates use their unique tracking links or promo codes to direct potential customers to the product's sales page. When a sale is made through their referral, the affiliate earns a predetermined commission, which is typically a percentage of the product's sale price.

One of the key benefits of affiliate products is that they offer a low-risk way for individuals to start an online business. Affiliates don't have to worry about creating their own products, managing inventory, or dealing with customer service issues. Instead, they can focus on promoting the products and earning commissions for each sale they generate.

Affiliate products also provide an opportunity for passive income. Once affiliates have set up their marketing channels and established a steady stream of traffic, they can continue to earn commissions on sales without having to actively promote the products on a daily basis. This can lead to a scalable and potentially lucrative income stream over time.

In addition to physical and digital products, affiliate marketing also extends to services such as web hosting, online tools, and subscription-based memberships. These types of affiliate products often offer recurring commissions, allowing affiliates to earn ongoing income for as long as their referrals remain customers.

Affiliate products play a crucial role in the e-commerce ecosystem by enabling businesses to leverage the power of affiliate marketing to drive sales and expand their market reach. For affiliates, these products provide an accessible and flexible way to earn income online by promoting and selling a wide range of offerings across different industries and niches.

To effectively promote affiliate products and generate money through affiliate marketing, it is important to first identify a niche that aligns with your interests, expertise, and the needs of your target audience. Once you have chosen a niche, it is crucial to conduct thorough research to understand the products and services available in that niche, as well as the needs and preferences of your audience. This will enable you to select the most relevant and high-quality affiliate products to promote.

After selecting the affiliate products, the next step is to create valuable and engaging content that showcases the benefits and features of the products. This can be done through various channels such as a blog, social media, email marketing, or video content. The key is to provide informative and compelling content that educates and persuades your audience to consider purchasing the affiliate products.

In addition to creating content, it is essential to build a strong and trustworthy relationship with your audience. This can be achieved by engaging with them regularly; addressing their concerns and questions, and providing genuine recommendations based on your own experiences with the affiliate products. Building trust with your audience will increase the likelihood of them making a purchase through your affiliate links.

Another effective strategy to promote affiliate products is to leverage the power of search engine optimization (SEO) to drive organic traffic to your content. By optimizing your content with relevant keywords, creating high-quality back-links, and providing valuable information, you can improve your visibility on search engines and attract more potential customers to your affiliate links.

Furthermore, utilizing paid advertising can be a powerful way to promote affiliate products and reach a larger audience. Platforms such as Google Ads, Facebook Ads, and Instagram Ads allow you to target specific demographics and interests, enabling you to reach potential customers who are likely to be interested in the affiliate products you are promoting.

Collaborating with influencers and other content creators in your niche can also be an effective way to promote affiliate products. By partnering with individuals who have a large and engaged following, you can leverage their influence to reach a wider audience and drive more traffic to your affiliate links.

Additionally, offering incentives such as discounts, bonuses, or exclusive offers can incentivize your audience to make a purchase through your affiliate links. By providing additional value to your audience, you can increase their motivation to take action and generate more sales for the affiliate products you are promoting.

It is also important to continuously track and analyze the performance of your affiliate marketing efforts. By monitoring key metrics such as click-through rates, conversion rates, and sales, you can identify which strategies are most effective and make data-driven decisions to optimize your promotional activities.

Staying updated with the latest trends and developments in your niche and the affiliate marketing industry is crucial for staying competitive and maximizing your earning potential. By adapting to changes in consumer behaviour, technology, and market dynamics, you can refine your promotional strategies and continue to generate money through affiliate marketing.

Build an Email List:

In affiliate marketing, an email list is a crucial tool for building and maintaining relationships with potential customers. It is a collection of email addresses that have been voluntarily provided by individuals who are interested in a particular niche or product. These email addresses are typically obtained through opt-in forms on websites, landing pages, or through other means of lead generation. Once collected, the email list becomes a valuable asset for affiliate marketers as it allows them to communicate directly with their audience, promote products and services, and ultimately drive sales.

Building an email list is essential for affiliate marketers as it provides a direct line of communication with potential customers. By having an email list, marketers can send targeted messages to their subscribers, providing them with valuable content, product recommendations, and special offers. This direct communication allows affiliate marketers to build trust and rapport with their audience, leading to higher conversion rates and increased sales.

Moreover, an email list provides affiliate marketers with a way to nurture leads over time. Not all potential customers are ready to make a purchase immediately, and having an email list allows marketers to stay top-of-mind with their audience. By regularly sending valuable content and offers to their subscribers, affiliate marketers can keep their audience engaged and interested in the products or services they are promoting.

In addition, an email list allows affiliate marketers to segment their audience based on various criteria such as interests, buying behaviour, or demographics. This segmentation enables marketers to send highly targeted and personalized messages to different groups of subscribers, increasing the relevance and effectiveness of their marketing efforts.

Furthermore, an email list provides affiliate marketers with a way to measure the effectiveness of their marketing campaigns. By tracking metrics such as open rates, click-through rates, and conversion rates, marketers can gain valuable insights into the performance of their email campaigns and make data-driven decisions to optimize their strategies.

An email list also serves as a valuable asset for affiliate marketers as it provides them with a direct channel for promoting products and generating sales. By sending targeted promotions and offers to their subscribers, marketers can drive traffic to affiliate offers and earn commissions on resulting sales.

Additionally, an email list allows affiliate marketers to stay in compliance with anti-spam laws and regulations by obtaining explicit consent from subscribers before sending them marketing messages. This not only helps to maintain a positive reputation but also ensures that marketers are abiding by legal requirements.

Moreover, an email list provides affiliate marketers with a way to stay connected with their audience even if other marketing channels such as social media or search engines undergo changes or algorithm updates. By having a direct line of communication with their subscribers, marketers can maintain a level of control over their marketing efforts and reduce reliance on external platforms.

An email list is a fundamental component of affiliate marketing that allows marketers to build relationships, nurture leads, segment their audience, measure campaign effectiveness, promote products, stay compliant with regulations, and maintain control over their marketing efforts. It is an invaluable tool for driving sales and growing a successful affiliate marketing business.

<u>Email list is very important in marketing campaigns:</u>

Consider building an email list to engage with your audience and promote affiliate products through email marketing campaigns. This can be achieved by using auto responder software like;
(1). Get-response
(2). Aweber

GetResponse and AWeber are both essential tools for building an email list in affiliate marketing. These platforms provide the necessary infrastructure for creating and managing email campaigns, enabling affiliate marketers to effectively reach and engage with their target audience. By using these tools, affiliate marketers can automate the process of capturing leads, nurturing relationships, and promoting products or services to a highly targeted audience.

One of the key benefits of using GetResponse and AWeber is their ability to help affiliate marketers build a highly targeted email list. These platforms offer a range of tools and features that enable marketers to create customized opt-in forms, landing pages, and lead magnets that are designed to attract and capture the attention of potential subscribers. This targeted approach allows affiliate marketers to build a list of subscribers who are genuinely interested in the products or services being promoted, increasing the likelihood of conversion and sales.

Furthermore, GetResponse and AWeber provide powerful automation capabilities that allow affiliate marketers to streamline their email marketing efforts. These platforms offer features such as autoresponders, email sequencing, and behavioral triggers, which enable marketers to deliver personalized and timely messages to their subscribers. By automating these processes, affiliate marketers can save time and resources while ensuring that their subscribers receive relevant and engaging content that is tailored to their interests and needs.

In addition, GetResponse and AWeber offer advanced tracking and analytics tools that provide valuable insights into the performance of email campaigns. These platforms enable affiliate marketers to monitor key metrics such as open rates, click-through rates, and conversion rates, allowing them to optimize their campaigns for maximum effectiveness. By leveraging these insights, affiliate marketers can make data-driven decisions that improve the overall performance of their email marketing efforts.

Moreover, both GetResponse and AWeber offer integration with a wide range of third-party tools and services, enabling affiliate marketers to seamlessly connect their email marketing efforts with other aspects of their business. This integration allows marketers to leverage the power of email marketing in conjunction with other marketing channels, such as social media, content marketing, and paid advertising, creating a cohesive and multi-faceted approach to reaching and engaging with their target audience.

Another important aspect of using GetResponse and AWeber in building an email list in affiliate marketing is their compliance with industry regulations and best practices. These platforms are designed to ensure that marketers adhere to laws such as the CAN-SPAM Act and the General Data Protection Regulation (GDPR), protecting both the marketer and the subscriber. By using these platforms, affiliate marketers can maintain a positive reputation and build trust with their subscribers, ultimately leading to stronger relationships and higher conversion rates.

Furthermore, GetResponse and AWeber provide extensive support and resources to help affiliate marketers succeed in their email marketing efforts. These platforms offer comprehensive knowledge bases, tutorials, webinars, and customer support services that enable marketers to learn best practices, troubleshoot issues, and stay updated on the latest trends and developments in email marketing. This support empowers affiliate marketers to make the most of their email marketing efforts and achieve their business goals.

Additionally, using GetResponse and AWeber in building an email list in affiliate marketing enables marketers to leverage the power of segmentation and personalization. These platforms offer robust segmentation features that allow marketers to categorize their subscribers based on various criteria such as demographics, behavior, and interests. By segmenting their list, affiliate marketers can deliver highly targeted and relevant content to different groups of subscribers, increasing engagement and driving conversions.

In conclusion, the importance of using GetResponse and AWeber in building an email list in affiliate marketing cannot be overstated. These platforms provide the essential tools and features that enable affiliate marketers to build, manage, and optimize their email campaigns for maximum effectiveness. By leveraging the capabilities of these platforms, affiliate marketers can build a highly targeted list of subscribers, automate their email marketing efforts, gain valuable insights through analytics, integrate with other marketing channels, ensure compliance with regulations, access extensive support and resources, and leverage segmentation and personalization to drive engagement and conversions.

Track Performance:

Track performance in affiliate marketing is crucial for both advertisers and publishers. It involves monitoring and analyzing various metrics to evaluate the effectiveness of marketing campaigns and the overall success of affiliate partnerships. Performance tracking allows advertisers to measure the return on investment (ROI) of their affiliate programs, while publishers can assess the performance of their marketing efforts and optimize their strategies for better results.

One key aspect of track performance in affiliate marketing is monitoring conversion rates. This involves tracking the number of clicks on affiliate links that result in desired actions, such as a sale or a lead. By analyzing conversion rates, advertisers can identify which affiliates are driving the most valuable traffic and which marketing channels are delivering the best results. Publishers can also use this data to optimize their promotional tactics and focus on high-converting traffic sources.

Another important metric to track in affiliate marketing is the average order value (AOV). This metric helps advertisers and publishers understand the average amount of revenue generated from each sale driven by affiliate traffic. By monitoring AOV, advertisers can identify opportunities to increase sales value, while publishers can focus on promoting products or services with higher AOV to maximize their earnings.

Tracking customer acquisition costs (CAC) is also essential in affiliate marketing. This metric helps advertisers understand how much it costs to acquire a new customer through affiliate channels. By comparing CAC with the lifetime value of customers, advertisers can determine the profitability of their affiliate programs and make informed decisions about commission rates and marketing budgets.

In addition to tracking financial metrics, it's important to monitor engagement and retention metrics in affiliate marketing. This includes tracking metrics such as click-through rates, bounce rates, and customer retention rates. By analyzing these metrics, advertisers and publishers can gain insights into the quality of traffic driven by affiliates and identify opportunities to improve user experience and customer loyalty.

Furthermore, tracking performance in affiliate marketing involves monitoring and analyzing data from multiple sources, including affiliate networks, tracking platforms, and analytics tools. This requires implementing robust tracking systems and using advanced analytics to gather and interpret data accurately. Advertisers and publishers need to ensure that they have the right technology and expertise to track performance effectively and make data-driven decisions.
Moreover, track performance in affiliate marketing also involves monitoring the compliance and quality of affiliate traffic. Advertisers need to ensure that affiliates adhere to ethical marketing practices and comply with relevant regulations. Publishers need to monitor the quality of traffic to maintain a positive reputation and build trust with advertisers and customers.

Track performance in affiliate marketing is essential for measuring the success of marketing campaigns, optimizing strategies, and maximizing the return on investment. By monitoring key metrics such as conversion rates, average order value, customer acquisition costs, and engagement metrics, advertisers and publishers can make informed decisions to drive growth and profitability in their affiliate partnerships. Effective performance tracking requires the use of advanced technology, robust tracking systems, and data analysis skills to gather actionable insights and drive continuous improvement in affiliate marketing efforts.

Use click tracking tools provided by affiliate programs to monitor the performance of your affiliate links. Analyze click-through rates, conversions, and earnings to optimize your promotional strategies. Click tracking tools are analytics software that help website owners track the behaviour of their users. They can be used to track a variety of metrics, including the number of clicks on a particular link, the number of times a user visits a particular page, and the amount of time a user spends on a particular page.

Click tracking tools can be used to improve the user experience of a website by identifying areas where users are having difficulty navigating or finding the information they need. They can also be used to optimize marketing campaigns by tracking the effectiveness of different ad campaigns and landing pages.

There are many different clicks tracking tools available, both free and paid. Some of the most popular click tracking tools includes Google Analytics, Clicky, and Hotjar.

To use a click tracking tool, you will need to install a small piece of code on your website. This code will track the behaviour of your users and send the data to the click tracking tool's servers. You can then use the click tracking tool's dashboard to view the data and generate reports.

Click tracking tools can be a valuable asset for website owners who want to improve the user experience of their website and optimize their marketing campaigns.

Engage with Your Audience:

Engaging with the audience in affiliate marketing is crucial for success in this competitive industry. One effective way to engage with your audience is by creating high-quality, valuable content that resonates with their needs and interests. This can be achieved through blog posts, social media updates, videos, podcasts, or any other form of content that your audience prefers. By consistently providing valuable content, you can build trust and credibility with your audience, which can lead to increased engagement and conversions.

Another important aspect of engaging with your audience in affiliate marketing is to actively listen to their feedback and respond to their comments and questions. This can be done through social media, email, or even in-person events. By showing that you value their input and are willing to address their concerns, you can foster a sense of community and connection with your audience.

In addition to creating valuable content and actively listening to your audience, it's also important to personalize your interactions with them. This can be achieved by addressing them by name in your communications, tailoring your content to their specific needs and interests, and showing genuine interest in their lives and experiences. By making your audience feel seen and heard, you can strengthen the bond between you and them, leading to increased engagement and loyalty.

Furthermore, engaging with your audience in affiliate marketing involves building a sense of exclusivity and belonging. This can be achieved by offering special promotions, discounts, or insider access to your audience. By making them feel like they are part of an exclusive club, you can create a sense of loyalty and excitement around your brand and offers.

Moreover, engaging with your audience in affiliate marketing also involves being transparent and honest in your communications. This means disclosing your affiliate relationships and being upfront about any potential biases in your recommendations. By being transparent, you can build trust with your audience and ensure that they feel confident in the products or services you promote.

Additionally, engaging with your audience in affiliate marketing requires being responsive and accessible. This means being available to answer their questions, address their concerns, and provide support when needed. By being responsive and accessible, you can show your audience that you are committed to their satisfaction and success, which can lead to increased engagement and conversions.

Another effective way to engage with your audience in affiliate marketing is by leveraging user-generated content. Encourage your audience to share their experiences with the products or services you promote, and showcase their testimonials, reviews, or success stories. By highlighting the experiences of real customers, you can build social proof and credibility around the products or services you promote.

Engaging with your audience in affiliate marketing involves creating interactive experiences that encourage participation and engagement. This can be achieved through contests, polls, quizzes, or live Q&A sessions. By creating interactive experiences, you can capture the attention of your audience and encourage them to actively engage with your brand and offers.

Engaging with your audience in affiliate marketing involves building long-term relationships based on mutual trust and respect. This means consistently providing value, being authentic and genuine in your communications, and always putting the needs of your audience first. By building long-term relationships, you can create a loyal and engaged audience that continues to support and advocate for your brand.

Diversify Your Promotions:

When it comes to diversifying your promotions in affiliate marketing, it's important to explore various channels and tactics to reach a wider audience and maximize your earning potential. One way to diversify your promotions is by leveraging different social media platforms. For example, you can create engaging content on Instagram, Facebook, Twitter, and Pinterest to showcase the products or services you are promoting. Each platform has its own unique features and audience demographics, so tailoring your content to each platform can help you reach a diverse group of potential customers.

Another effective way to diversify your promotions is by utilizing email marketing. Building an email list allows you to directly communicate with your audience and promote various affiliate offers. You can segment your email list based on different interests or buying behaviours, allowing you to send targeted promotions that are more likely to resonate with your subscribers.

In addition to social media and email marketing, you can also diversify your promotions by creating valuable content such as blog posts, videos, or podcasts. By providing informative and engaging content related to the products or services you are promoting, you can attract organic traffic and build trust with your audience. This can lead to higher conversion rates and increased affiliate earnings.

Furthermore, collaborating with influencers or other affiliates can help diversify your promotions. Partnering with individuals who have a large and engaged following can expose your promotions to new audiences and provide valuable social proof. Additionally, working with other affiliates can lead to joint promotions or cross-promotional opportunities, allowing you to tap into each other's networks and expand your reach.

Another strategy to diversify your promotions is by utilizing paid advertising. Platforms such as Google Ads, Facebook Ads, and native advertising networks offer a variety of targeting options that allow you to reach specific demographics or interests. By investing in paid advertising, you can complement your organic promotional efforts and potentially reach a wider audience that may not have been exposed to your promotions otherwise.

Moreover, participating in affiliate networks or programs can also help diversify your promotions. These networks often have a wide range of offers across different industries, allowing you to promote diverse products or services to your audience. Additionally, some affiliate networks offer exclusive deals or higher commission rates, providing you with more opportunities to diversify your promotional efforts.

Furthermore, optimizing your website for search engines (SEO) can also diversify your promotions by attracting organic traffic. By creating high-quality content and optimizing your website for relevant keywords, you can attract visitors who are actively searching for the products or services you are promoting. This can result in more qualified leads and higher conversion rates.

Additionally, leveraging emerging technologies such as chatbots or voice search can also diversify your promotions. Chatbots can engage with visitors in real-time and provide personalized recommendations, while optimizing for voice search can help you capture traffic from users who are utilizing voice-activated devices such as smart speakers or smartphones.

Continuously testing and analyzing the performance of your promotions is crucial for diversification. By tracking key metrics such as click-through rates, conversion rates, and customer acquisition costs, you can identify which channels or tactics are most effective and allocate your resources accordingly. This data-driven approach can help you refine your promotional strategies and continually optimize for better results.

Stay Informed: Stay updated on industry trends, new product launches, and changes in affiliate programs. Adapt your strategies based on market developments.

Generating income through affiliate marketing is cost effective as you can start today freely without monetary investing by just joining affiliate related companies like clickbank.com.

Chapter 6
Creating and Monetizing a YouTube Channel.

A YouTube channel is a dedicated space on the YouTube platform where users can upload, organize, and share videos with a global audience. It serves as a personalized hub for content creators to showcase their videos, engage with viewers, and build a community around their content.

Creating and monetizing a YouTube channel involves the process of establishing a channel on the YouTube platform, producing and uploading content, and earning revenue through various monetization features offered by YouTube. Here's a breakdown of the key steps involved in creating and monetizing a YouTube channel:

When choosing a YouTube channel, there are several factors to consider in order to find the best fit for your interests and preferences. First and foremost, it's important to identify your own personal interests and hobbies. Consider what topics you are passionate about and what type of content you enjoy consuming. Whether it's cooking, gaming, fashion, or travel, there are countless channels catering to a wide range of interests.

Once you have identified your interests, take some time to explore different channels within those categories. Look for channels that have a strong and engaging presence, high-quality production value, and a consistent upload schedule. It's also important to consider the personality of the content creator and whether their style resonates with you. Some creators have a more casual and conversational approach, while others may have a more polished and professional demeanours.

Another important factor to consider when choosing a YouTube channel is the type of content that is being produced. Do you prefer informative and educational videos, entertaining vlogs, or in-depth tutorials? Consider the format and style of the content to ensure that it aligns with your preferences. Additionally, take note of the length of the videos and whether they fit within your desired viewing time.

In addition to the content itself, it's important to consider the community and engagement surrounding the channel. Look for channels that foster a positive and supportive community, where viewers can interact with each other and with the content creator. Pay attention to the comments section and social media presence to gauge the level of engagement and interaction.

Furthermore, consider the credibility and expertise of the content creator. Look for channels where the creator has a strong knowledge base and experience within their niche. Whether it's a beauty guru sharing makeup tips or a tech expert reviewing the latest gadgets, credibility and expertise are important factors to consider when choosing a YouTube channel.

It's also important to take into account the frequency of uploads and consistency of content. Look for channels that regularly produce new content and maintain a consistent schedule. This ensures that you have a steady stream of videos to watch and helps you stay engaged with the channel.

Reflect on the production quality of the videos as well. Look for channels that have high-quality visuals, clear audio, and professional editing. A well-produced video can greatly enhance the viewing experience and make the content more enjoyable to watch.

Another important aspect to consider is the diversity of content on the channel. Look for channels that offer a variety of content within your chosen interest or niche. Whether it's different types of recipes on a cooking channel or various workout routines on a fitness channel, having diverse content can keep the channel fresh and engaging.

Creating high-quality content for your YouTube channel requires careful planning and attention to detail. To start, it's important to identify your target audience and understand their interests and preferences. This will help you tailor your content to meet their needs and keep them engaged. Additionally, it's crucial to stay up-to-date with current trends and topics that are relevant to your niche in order to produce content that is both timely and valuable to your viewers.

Another key aspect of creating high-quality content is to ensure that it is visually appealing. This includes using high-quality cameras and equipment to capture crisp, clear footage. Additionally, paying attention to lighting, framing, and composition can greatly enhance the overall production value of your videos. Investing in professional editing software can also help you create polished, professional-looking content that will keep your viewers coming back for more.

In addition to visual appeal, it's important to focus on creating content that is both informative and entertaining. This can be achieved by delivering valuable information in a compelling and engaging manner. Whether it's through storytelling, demonstrations, or interviews, finding creative ways to present your content can help captivate your audience and keep them coming back for more.

Consistency is also key when it comes to creating high-quality content for your YouTube channel. This means establishing a regular posting schedule and sticking to it. This not only helps build anticipation among your audience, but it also demonstrates your commitment to delivering valuable content on a consistent basis.

Furthermore, engaging with your audience is essential for creating high-quality content. This can be done by responding to comments, asking for feedback, and incorporating viewer suggestions into your content. Building a community around your channel can help foster loyalty among your audience and keep them actively engaged with your content.

Moreover, collaborating with other creators in your niche can help you expand your reach and bring fresh perspectives to your content. By partnering with like-minded creators, you can tap into each other's audiences and create content that is mutually beneficial.

It's also important to stay authentic and true to yourself when creating content for your YouTube channel. Your unique voice and perspective are what make your channel stand out, so don't be afraid to let your personality shine through in your videos.

Staying open to feedback and continuously seeking ways to improve your content is crucial for maintaining high quality. This can involve analyzing your performance metrics, seeking input from your audience, and staying open to new ideas and approaches that can help elevate the quality of your content.

Creating high-quality content for your YouTube channel requires a combination of careful planning, creativity, and a commitment to delivering value to your audience. By staying true to your unique voice, engaging with your audience, and continuously seeking ways to improve, you can create content that resonates with viewers and sets your channel apart.

Optimizations of videos are very vital; to optimize your videos on your YouTube channel, it's important to start with keyword research. Use tools like Google Keyword Planner or YouTube's own search suggest feature to find relevant keywords that have high search volume but low competition. Incorporate these keywords naturally into your video titles, descriptions, and tags to increase the likelihood of your videos being discovered by potential viewers.

Next, focus on creating engaging and high-quality content. YouTube's algorithm prioritizes videos that keep viewers on the platform for longer periods of time, so aim to create videos that are entertaining, informative, and visually appealing. Consider using a hook at the beginning of your videos to capture viewers' attention and encourage them to keep watching.

In addition to creating great content, it's important to optimize your video metadata. This includes writing compelling video titles and descriptions that accurately represent the content of your videos. Use relevant keywords in your titles and descriptions, but make sure they are written for humans first and foremost. Additionally, use tags to further categorize your videos and make them more discoverable to potential viewers.

Another important aspect of optimizing your videos on YouTube is to create custom thumbnails. Thumbnails are often the first thing potential viewers see when browsing through videos, so it's important to create eye-catching and high-quality thumbnails that accurately represent the content of your videos. Use bright colours, clear images, and text overlays to make your thumbnails stand out.

It's also important to promote your videos across other platforms to increase their visibility. Share your videos on social media, embed them in blog posts, and include them in email newsletters to reach a wider audience. Additionally, consider collaborating with other YouTubers or influencers in your niche to cross-promote each other's content.

Furthermore, engage with your audience by responding to comments and encouraging viewers to like, share, and subscribe to your channel. YouTube's algorithm takes into account engagement metrics like likes, comments, and shares, so actively encouraging these actions can help boost the visibility of your videos.

In addition to optimizing individual videos, it's important to maintain a consistent upload schedule. Regularly uploading new content signals to YouTube that your channel is active and can help improve your videos' visibility in search results and recommendations.

Analyze your video performance using YouTube analytics. Pay attention to metrics like watch time, audience retention, and click-through rate to understand how viewers are engaging with your content. Use this data to refine your content strategy and make informed decisions about future video topics and formats. By continuously optimizing your videos based on performance data, you can improve the overall success of your YouTube channel.

Building an audience for your YouTube channel requires a strategic approach and consistent effort. The first step is to define your target audience and create content that resonates with them. Research the demographics, interests, and preferences of your potential viewers to tailor your content to their needs. Understanding your audience will help you create engaging and relevant videos that will attract and retain subscribers.

Consistency is the key to building an audience on YouTube. Regularly uploading high-quality content will keep your viewers engaged and encourage them to subscribe to your channel. Develop a content schedule and stick to it to establish a sense of reliability and dependability with your audience. Consistent uploads will also signal to the YouTube algorithm that your channel is active and relevant, increasing the likelihood of your videos being recommended to new viewers.

Engaging with your audience is crucial for building a loyal fan base. Respond to comments, ask for feedback, and encourage viewers to participate in discussions. Building a community around your channel will create a sense of belonging and connection, making viewers more likely to subscribe and return for future content. Show genuine interest in your audience's opinions and make them feel valued, which will foster a strong and dedicated following.

Collaborating with other YouTubers can help expose your channel to new audiences and attract more subscribers. Look for creators in your niche or related fields and propose collaboration ideas that benefit both parties. Cross-promoting each other's channels and appearing in each other's videos can introduce your content to a wider audience and increase your subscriber count. Collaborations also provide opportunities for creative input and fresh perspectives, adding diversity to your content and attracting new viewers.

Utilize social media platforms to promote your YouTube channel and engage with potential subscribers. Share teasers, behind-the-scenes content, and updates about upcoming videos on platforms like Instagram, Twitter, and Facebook to generate interest and drive traffic to your channel. Engage with your followers on social media, respond to their messages, and encourage them to check out your YouTube content. Leveraging social media can expand your reach and attract new subscribers from different online communities.

Optimizing your videos for search engines is essential for attracting new viewers to your channel. Conduct keyword research to identify popular search terms related to your content and incorporate them into your video titles, descriptions, and tags. This will increase the visibility of your videos in search results and make it easier for potential subscribers to discover your channel. Additionally, creating compelling thumbnails and writing attention-grabbing video titles can entice viewers to click on your videos and subscribe to your channel.

Offering value to your audience is crucial for building a loyal subscriber base. Create content that educates, entertains, or inspires viewers, providing them with something valuable in return for their time and attention. Whether it's sharing useful tips, telling engaging stories, or showcasing unique talents, focus on delivering content that enriches the lives of your audience. When viewers perceive the value in your videos, they are more likely to subscribe and become dedicated fans of your channel.

Hosting live streams or Q&A sessions can help you connect with your audience in real-time and foster a sense of community on your channel. Live interactions allow viewers to engage with you directly, ask questions, and share their thoughts, creating a more personal and intimate experience. Hosting regular live sessions can build anticipation among your audience and encourage them to subscribe to ensure they don't miss out on the opportunity to interact with you in real-time. Live streams also provide an opportunity to showcase your personality and build a stronger connection with your viewers.

Analyze your channel's performance using YouTube analytics to understand what resonates with your audience and adjust your content strategy accordingly. Pay attention to metrics like watch time, audience retention, and subscriber growth to identify trends and patterns in viewer behaviour. Use this data to refine your content strategy, optimize future videos, and tailor your approach to better meet the needs and preferences of your audience. By continuously learning from your analytics, you can refine your content strategy and attract more subscribers to your channel.

Enable monetization on your YouTube channel and start making money, the first step is to meet the eligibility requirements set by YouTube. This includes having at least 1,000 subscribers on your channel and accumulating 4,000 watch hours in the past 12 months. Once you meet these requirements, you can apply for the YouTube Partner Program through your YouTube account.

After applying for the YouTube Partner Program, your channel will be reviewed to ensure it complies with YouTube's policies and guidelines. This review process can take some time, but once your channel is approved, you can start monetizing your videos. To do this, you'll need to enable monetization on your channel by going to the "Monetization" section in your YouTube Studio dashboard and following the prompts to set up an AdSense account.

Once your AdSense account is linked to your YouTube channel, you can start earning money from your videos through various monetization methods. This includes displaying ads on your videos, participating in the YouTube Partner Program, and utilizing other monetization features such as Super Chat, channel memberships, and merchandise shelf.

In addition to enabling monetization on your channel, it's important to create high-quality, engaging content that will attract viewers and keep them coming back for more. This can help increase your watch time and engagement, which are important factors in generating revenue on YouTube. You should also pay attention to your audience's interests and preferences, and tailor your content to meet their needs.

Another important aspect of monetizing your YouTube channel is promoting your videos and building a strong subscriber base. This can be done through various means such as sharing your videos on social media, collaborating with other YouTubers, and engaging with your audience through comments and community posts. Building a loyal fan base can help increase your video views and ultimately boost your earnings.

It's also important to stay up to date with YouTube's policies and guidelines to ensure that your content remains eligible for monetization. This includes avoiding copyright infringement, adhering to community guidelines, and staying informed about any changes or updates to YouTube's monetization policies.

Furthermore, you can optimize your videos for search by using relevant keywords, creating compelling thumbnails, and writing detailed video descriptions. This can help increase the visibility of your videos on YouTube and attract more viewers, which can ultimately lead to higher ad revenue and earnings for your channel.

In addition to ad revenue, you can explore other revenue streams on YouTube such as sponsorships, affiliate marketing, and selling digital or physical products. Diversifying your income streams can help maximize your earnings and make your YouTube channel more profitable in the long run.

Enabling monetization on your YouTube channel requires meeting eligibility requirements, creating high-quality content, promoting your videos, staying informed about YouTube's policies, and exploring various revenue streams. With dedication and perseverance, you can turn your passion for creating videos into a successful and lucrative business on YouTube.

Explore additional revenue streams on a YouTube channel and make money, creators can consider various strategies. One approach is to diversify content by creating and selling merchandise related to the channel. This could include branded clothing, accessories, or digital products such as e-books or online courses. By leveraging the existing audience and brand, creators can tap into the lucrative market of merchandise sales.

Another avenue for generating revenue is through sponsored content and brand partnerships. Collaborating with relevant companies and promoting their products or services in videos can be a lucrative source of income. Creators can negotiate sponsored deals directly with brands or work with influencer marketing platforms to connect with suitable partners.

Furthermore, YouTube creators can explore crowdfunding as a means to generate additional income. Platforms like Patreon or Ko-fi allow fans to support their favourite creators through monthly subscriptions or one-time donations. In exchange, creators can offer exclusive perks such as behind-the-scenes content, Q&A sessions, or early access to videos.

Additionally, creators can monetize their expertise by offering consulting services or coaching sessions. For example, fitness YouTuber could provide personalized training programs, while a finance channel could offer one-on-one financial planning sessions. This approach not only generates income but also establishes the creator as an authority in their niche.

Another potential revenue stream is affiliate marketing, where creators promote products or services and earn a commission on sales. By including affiliate links in video descriptions or dedicated recommendation videos, creators can monetize their recommendations and capitalize on their audience's trust.

Moreover, hosting live events or meetups can be a profitable endeavour for YouTube creators. Whether it's a ticketed workshop, fan convention, or exclusive meetup, in-person events provide an opportunity to connect with the audience and generate revenue through ticket sales, merchandise, and sponsorship's.

Additionally, creators can leverage their expertise to create and sell digital products such as e-books, online courses, or exclusive content. This allows them to monetize their knowledge and provide additional value to their audience.

YouTube creators can explore licensing opportunities for their content. This could involve selling footage to stock video platforms, licensing music or sound effects, or collaborating with brands to create sponsored content for their own marketing purposes.

Creators can consider expanding their presence on other platforms such as Patreon, Twitch, or even launching a podcast. By diversifying their online presence, creators can tap into new audiences and revenue streams while strengthening their brand and content offerings.

You want to promote your video on YouTube using affiliate marketing, there are several strategies you can employ to maximize your reach and engagement. First and foremost, it's important to choose the right affiliate programs that align with the content of your video and the interests of your audience. Look for programs that offer relevant products or services that your viewers are likely to be interested in. Once you've identified the right affiliate programs, you can incorporate affiliate links into your video description and encourage viewers to click on them to learn more about the products or services you're promoting.

Another effective way to promote your video using affiliate marketing is to create dedicated content around the products or services you're promoting. This could include product reviews, tutorials, or demonstrations that showcase the benefits and features of the affiliate products. By creating valuable and informative content, you can build trust with your audience and increase the likelihood that they will click on your affiliate links and make a purchase.

In addition to creating dedicated content, you can also leverage other marketing channels to promote your affiliate links. For example, you can share your video on social media platforms and include your affiliate links in your posts. You can also collaborate with other YouTubers or influencers in your niche to cross-promote each other's content and reach a wider audience. By expanding your reach beyond YouTube, you can increase the visibility of your affiliate links and drive more traffic to the products or services you're promoting.

More so, it's important to be transparent and authentic when promoting affiliate products on your YouTube channel. Disclose any affiliate relationships and be honest about your experiences with the products or services you're promoting. Your audience will appreciate your honesty and authenticity, which can ultimately lead to higher engagement and conversions.

Another effective strategy for promoting your video using affiliate marketing is to optimize your video content for search engines. By incorporating relevant keywords into your video titles, descriptions, and tags, you can improve the visibility of your videos in search results and attract more viewers who are actively looking for the products or services you're promoting. Additionally, you can create custom thumbnails and compelling titles that entice viewers to click on your videos and learn more about the affiliate products or services you're promoting.

It's also important to track the performance of your affiliate links and analyze the data to understand what's working and what's not. By monitoring metrics such as click-through rates, conversion rates, and sales, you can identify which strategies are most effective and optimize your approach accordingly. This data-driven approach can help you refine your affiliate marketing efforts and maximize the impact of your promotional activities.

Moreover, building a strong email list can be a powerful tool for promoting your affiliate links. By capturing the email addresses of your viewers, you can nurture relationships with them over time and promote relevant affiliate products or services through targeted email campaigns. Offering exclusive discounts or bonuses to subscribers can incentivize them to click on your affiliate links and make a purchase, driving additional revenue for your channel.

Consider offering incentives to encourage viewers to click on your affiliate links. This could include special discounts, bonus content, or giveaways for viewers who make a purchase through your affiliate links. By providing added value to your audience, you can increase the likelihood that they will take action on your recommendations and support your channel through affiliate purchases.

Promoting your video on YouTube using affiliate marketing requires a strategic and multi-faceted approach. By choosing the right affiliate programs, creating valuable content, leveraging other marketing channels, being transparent and authentic, optimizing for search engines, tracking performance, building an email list, and offering incentives, you can effectively promote your affiliate links and drive more revenue for your channel.

Branding partnerships can be a great way to add value to your videos and monetize your content. When looking for brand partners, it's important to consider companies that align with your audience and content. This will ensure that the partnership feels authentic and natural, rather than forced or out of place. It's also important to consider the values and reputation of the brand, as you don't want to be associated with a company that doesn't align with your own personal values or the values of your audience.

Once you've identified potential brand partners, it's important to reach out to them with a clear proposal. This should include information about your audience demographics, engagement metrics, and any relevant previous brand partnerships or endorsements. It's also important to outline what you can offer the brand in terms of exposure and promotion, whether it's through dedicated videos, product placements, or sponsored content.

When negotiating the terms of the partnership, it's important to be clear about what you expect from the brand and what they can expect from you. This includes details about payment, deliverables, and any exclusivity agreements. It's also important to ensure that the partnership is legally sound and that both parties are protected in case of any disputes or issues.

Once the partnership is established, it's important to integrate the brand into your content in a way that feels natural and authentic. This could include dedicated videos or segments that highlight the brand's products or services, as well as subtle product placements or endorsements within your regular content. It's important to strike a balance between promoting the brand and maintaining the integrity of your content and relationship with your audience.

Throughout the partnership, it's important to maintain open communication with the brand to ensure that both parties are satisfied with the arrangement. This includes providing regular updates on performance metrics and engagement, as well as addressing any concerns or issues that may arise. It's also important to be flexible and adaptable, as the needs and goals of the brand may change over time.

After the partnership is completed, it's important to evaluate its success and impact on your content and audience. This could include analyzing engagement metrics, feedback from your audience, and any direct impact on your revenue or growth. It's also important to collect feedback from the brand partner to understand their perspective and any areas for improvement in future partnerships.

Overall, branding partnerships can be a valuable way to add value to your videos and monetize your content. By carefully selecting brand partners, negotiating clear terms, integrating the brand into your content authentically, and maintaining open communication throughout the partnership, you can create successful and mutually beneficial relationships that enhance your content and provide value to both you and the brand partner.

To analyze performance and be consistent in video production, it is essential to establish clear objectives and key performance indicators (KPIs) for each video project. This involves defining the purpose of the video, identifying the target audience, and setting specific goals such as engagement metrics, view counts, or conversion rates. By clearly defining what success looks like for each video, it becomes easier to measure performance and identify areas for improvement.

Another important aspect of analyzing performance in video production is to track and measure relevant metrics. This can include using tools like Google Analytics, YouTube Analytics, or social media insights to monitor key metrics such as views, watch time, engagement, and audience demographics. By regularly reviewing these metrics, it becomes possible to identify trends, understand what content resonates with the audience, and make data-driven decisions to improve performance.

Consistency in video production is crucial for building a strong brand and audience loyalty. This involves maintaining a consistent style, tone, and quality across all videos to create a cohesive and recognizable brand identity. It also means establishing a regular publishing schedule to keep the audience engaged and coming back for more content. Consistency can also apply to the overall production process, including using the same equipment, editing style, and production team to ensure a uniform and professional look and feel across all videos.

In order to maintain consistency in video production, it is important to create a detailed production plan for each video project. This plan should outline the overall concept, script, shooting schedule, editing timeline, and distribution strategy. By having a clear roadmap for each video, it becomes easier to stay organized, meet deadlines, and ensure that all videos align with the brand's overall vision and messaging.

Feedback and audience engagement are also essential for analyzing performance and maintaining consistency in video production. This can involve actively seeking feedback from viewers, monitoring comments and social media interactions, and conducting surveys or polls to gather insights into what the audience likes and dislikes. By listening to the audience and incorporating their feedback into future videos, it becomes possible to continuously improve performance and deliver content that resonates with the target audience.

Collaboration and teamwork are crucial for maintaining consistency in video production. This involves working closely with a dedicated team of professionals including videographers, editors, writers, and graphic designers to ensure that each video meets the highest standards of quality and aligns with the brand's overall vision. By fostering a collaborative environment, it becomes possible to leverage the unique skills and perspectives of each team member to create compelling and consistent video content.

Regularly reviewing and optimizing the production process is essential for maintaining consistency in video production. This can involve conducting post-mortem reviews after each video project to identify areas for improvement, streamline workflows, and implement best practices for future projects. By continuously refining the production process, it becomes possible to eliminate inefficiencies, reduce errors, and ensure that each video meets the brand's quality standards.

Staying up-to-date with industry trends and best practices is essential for analyzing performance and maintaining consistency in video production. This involves staying informed about the latest video formats, editing techniques, distribution platforms, and audience preferences. By staying ahead of the curve, it becomes possible to adapt to changing trends, leverage new opportunities, and deliver content that remains relevant and engaging to the target audience.

It is important to remain adaptable and open to change in order to analyze performance and maintain consistency in video production. This can involve being willing to experiment with new ideas, take calculated risks, and pivot strategies based on performance data and audience feedback. By remaining flexible and responsive to changes in the industry and audience preferences, it becomes possible to continuously improve performance and deliver high-quality video content that consistently resonates with the target audience.

Chapter 7
Developing and Selling Online Courses:

Online courses, also known as e-learning or distance learning, refer to educational courses that are conducted over the internet. These courses can be accessed from anywhere with an internet connection, allowing students to learn at their own pace and convenience. Online courses can cover a wide range of subjects, from academic disciplines to professional development and vocational training. They can be offered by traditional educational institutions, as well as by online learning platforms and individual instructors.

One defining characteristic of online courses is the use of digital technology to deliver course materials and facilitate communication between students and instructors. This can include video lectures, interactive multimedia content, online discussion forums, and virtual classroom sessions. Online courses may also incorporate various forms of assessment, such as quizzes, exams, and assignments, which are typically completed and submitted online.

Online courses offer flexibility and accessibility, making education more convenient for individuals with busy schedules or other commitments. Students can often access course materials and participate in discussions at any time of day, allowing them to fit their studies around work, family, or other responsibilities. Additionally, online courses can eliminate geographical barriers, enabling students from different locations to learn together without the need for physical travel.

Another key aspect of online courses is the potential for personalized learning experiences. With the use of digital tools and learning management systems, instructors can track students' progress, provide individualized feedback, and tailor course content to meet the needs of diverse learners. This adaptability can accommodate different learning styles and abilities, creating a more inclusive educational environment.

Online courses also promote self-discipline and independent learning skills. Without the structure of traditional classroom settings, students must take more responsibility for managing their time, staying motivated, and staying organized. This can help develop valuable attributes such as self-motivation, time management, and digital literacy, which are increasingly important in today's technology-driven society.

Furthermore, online courses can offer cost-effective alternatives to traditional education. By eliminating the need for physical facilities and reducing overhead expenses, online learning providers can often offer courses at lower tuition rates. Additionally, students can save money on commuting, housing, and other related expenses, making education more affordable and accessible to a wider range of individuals.

Online courses also have the potential to foster a global learning community. Through online discussions and collaborative projects, students from different backgrounds and cultures can engage in meaningful interactions and gain diverse perspectives. This can contribute to a more enriched learning experience and help prepare students for an increasingly interconnected and interdependent world.

Despite these advantages, online courses also present challenges and limitations. Some students may struggle with the lack of face-to-face interaction and the potential for feelings of isolation. Technical issues, such as unreliable internet connections or unfamiliarity with digital tools, can also hinder the learning experience for some individuals. Additionally, the quality and credibility of online courses can vary widely, requiring careful evaluation and discernment on the part of students.

Online courses offer a flexible, accessible, and potentially cost-effective approach to education that leverages digital technology to deliver personalized learning experiences. While they present opportunities for self-directed learning and global collaboration, they also come with unique challenges that require careful consideration. As technology continues to advance and reshape the educational landscape, online courses are likely to play an increasingly prominent role in meeting the diverse learning needs of students around the world.

Developing and selling online courses can be a lucrative way to share your expertise and knowledge with a broad audience. By developing and selling online courses, you can leverage your expertise to create valuable educational content that provides a source of income while helping learners acquire new skills and knowledge. These include creating educational content and offering it to learners through an online platform for a fee or free while increasing your mailing list and charging money via training platforms. Here's an overview of the process and key considerations for monetizing online courses:

Here are the steps to make money by developing and selling online courses:

Identify Your Expertise:

Identifying your expertise in developing and selling online courses involves a combination of self-reflection, market research, and skill assessment. First, take the time to reflect on your own experiences, knowledge, and passions. Consider what subjects or skills you are particularly knowledgeable about and passionate about sharing with others. This could be anything from cooking and nutrition to digital marketing or graphic design. Your expertise could also stem from your professional background, such as teaching experience or industry-specific knowledge.

Next, conduct market research to identify potential gaps or opportunities in the online course market. Look for popular topics that are in demand but may have limited competition. Consider conducting surveys or interviews with your target audience to better understand their needs and preferences. Additionally, analyze existing online courses to identify areas where you can offer a unique value proposition or a different approach that sets you apart from the competition.

Once you have a better understanding of your own expertise and the market demand, assess your skills in course development and sales. This could include instructional design, content creation, video production, marketing, and sales. Evaluate your strengths and weaknesses in each of these areas and consider seeking additional training or support in areas where you may need to improve.

Another important aspect of identifying your expertise in developing and selling online courses is to consider your target audience. Understand who your ideal students are and what they are looking for in an online course. Tailor your expertise and course offerings to meet the specific needs and preferences of your target audience to maximize your success.

It's also important to consider the format and delivery method of your online courses. Are you more comfortable with live webinars, pre-recorded video lessons, interactive quizzes, or a combination of these? Your expertise in course development should align with the format that best suits your teaching style and the preferences of your target audience.

Furthermore, consider leveraging your existing network and connections to validate your expertise and gain initial traction in selling your online courses. Seek endorsements or testimonials from colleagues, industry experts, or previous students to build credibility and trust with potential customers.

As you continue to develop and sell online courses, gather feedback from your students and use it to continuously improve and refine your offerings. This ongoing process of self-assessment and improvement will help you further establish and solidify your expertise in the field of online course development and sales.

Also consider seeking out mentorship or networking opportunities within the online course development and sales community. Learning from others who have already found success in this space can provide valuable insights and guidance as you continue to grow and develop your own expertise in this field.

Research Audience Demand:

When researching audience demand for developing and selling online courses, it's important to start by identifying a niche or target audience. This involves understanding the demographics, interests, and pain points of potential learners. Conducting surveys, interviews, and analyzing social media data can provide valuable insights into what potential students are looking for in an online course. By understanding the audience's needs and preferences, course creators can tailor their content to meet those needs and stand out in a crowded market.

Another important aspect of researching audience demand is to analyze keyword search volume and trends related to the topic of the course. Using tools like Google Keyword Planner or SEMrush can help identify popular search terms and topics within a specific niche. This can give course creators an idea of what topics are in high demand and what potential students are searching for online.

In addition to keyword research, analyzing competition can also provide valuable insights into audience demand. Understanding what other courses are available in the market, their pricing, and their strengths and weaknesses can help course creators identify gaps and opportunities to differentiate their own offerings. This competitive analysis can also reveal which courses are performing well and what aspects of those courses are resonating with the audience.

Engaging with potential students through online communities, forums, and social media platforms can also provide valuable qualitative insights into audience demand. By participating in discussions and asking questions, course creators can gain a deeper understanding of the challenges and aspirations of their target audience. This direct engagement can also help build relationships with potential students and create a sense of community around the course before it's even launched.

Utilizing data analytics tools to track website traffic, user behavior, and conversion rates can also provide valuable information about audience demand. By analyzing which pages are most visited, where users are dropping off, and which calls-to-action are most effective, course creators can gain insights into what resonates with their audience and what areas need improvement.

Conducting pilot tests or offering free mini-courses can also be a valuable way to gauge audience demand. By offering a small portion of the course content for free, course creators can gather feedback, testimonials, and data on engagement and completion rates. This can help validate the demand for the course before investing in its full development.

Lastly, staying updated on industry trends, changes in technology, and shifts in consumer behaviour is crucial for understanding audience demand. By keeping a pulse on the latest developments in the industry, course creators can anticipate future demand and adapt their offerings to meet evolving needs.

In conclusion, researching audience demand for developing and selling online courses involves a multi-faceted approach that combines quantitative data analysis with qualitative insights from direct engagement with potential students. By understanding the needs, preferences, and behaviours of the target audience, course creators can develop courses that resonate with learners and stand out in a competitive market.

Plan Your Course Content:

When planning your course content for developing and selling online courses, it's important to start by identifying your target audience. Understanding who your potential students are will help you tailor your content to their needs and preferences. Consider their background, level of expertise, and learning goals to create a course that resonates with them.

Next, conduct thorough research on the topic you plan to teach. Look for the latest trends, best practices, and relevant resources to ensure that your course content is up-to-date and valuable to your students. Consider incorporating different formats such as videos, quizzes, and downloadable resources to cater to various learning styles and enhance engagement.

Once you have a clear understanding of your audience and topic, outline the learning objectives for your course. What do you want your students to achieve by the end of the course? Setting clear and measurable learning outcomes will guide the development of your content and help students understand what they can expect to gain from the course.

After defining the learning objectives, organize your course content into logical modules or sections. This will help students navigate through the material more effectively and create a structured learning experience. Consider breaking down complex topics into smaller, digestible chunks to make the content more manageable and easier to comprehend.

Incorporate interactive elements into your course content to keep students engaged and motivated. This could include interactive quizzes, discussions, or assignments that encourage active participation and reinforce learning. Interactive elements can also help create a sense of community among students, fostering a supportive learning environment.

Consider offering supplementary resources and bonus materials to enrich the learning experience for your students. This could include additional readings, case studies, or practical exercises that complement the main course content and provide further value to your students. Providing extra resources can also help differentiate your course from others in the market.

As you develop your course content, keep in mind the importance of maintaining a balance between depth and accessibility. Ensure that the content is comprehensive enough to provide valuable insights and knowledge, but also presented in a way that is easy to understand for students with varying levels of expertise.

Before finalizing your course content, consider conducting a pilot test with a small group of students to gather feedback and identify areas for improvement. This will allow you to make necessary adjustments and ensure that the content meets the needs and expectations of your target audience before launching the course to a wider audience.

More so, when selling your online course, clearly communicate the value proposition of your content to potential students. Highlight the unique benefits and outcomes they can expect to achieve by enrolling in your course, and leverage testimonials or case studies from previous students to build credibility and trust. A compelling sales pitch can significantly impact the success of your course in a competitive market.

Choose a Platform:

When choosing a platform for developing and selling online courses, it's important to consider your specific needs and goals. One of the first things to consider is the type of content you'll be creating. Are you looking to create video-based courses, text-based courses, or a combination of both? Different platforms offer different features and capabilities, so it's important to choose one that aligns with the type of content you'll be creating.

Another important consideration is the level of customization and branding you require. Some platforms offer more flexibility in terms of customizing the look and feel of your courses, while others may be more limited in this regard. If branding is important to you, it's essential to choose a platform that allows you to create a consistent and professional brand experience for your students.

It's also important to consider the technical capabilities of the platform. Do you need features such as quizzes, assignments, discussion forums, or certificates? Make sure to choose a platform that offers the features and functionality you need to create an engaging and interactive learning experience for your students.

Consider the marketing and sales tools offered by the platform. Does it provide tools for promoting your courses, such as email marketing integrations, affiliate programs, or built-in sales pages? Choosing a platform with robust marketing and sales tools can help you reach a wider audience and maximize your course sales.

Another important factor to consider is the pricing and fees associated with the platform. Some platforms charge a monthly fee, while others take a percentage of your course sales. Make sure to choose a platform with pricing that aligns with your budget and revenue goals.

Consider the level of support and resources provided by the platform. Does it offer customer support, training resources, and a community of other course creators? Having access to support and resources can be invaluable as you navigate the process of creating and selling online courses.

It's also important to consider the scalability of the platform. As your business grows, will the platform be able to accommodate your needs? Choose a platform that can grow with you and provide the flexibility and scalability you need to expand your course offerings.

Consider the user experience for both you as the course creator and for your students. Is the platform easy to use and navigate? Does it provide a seamless and intuitive learning experience for your students? Choosing a platform that prioritizes user experience can help ensure that both you and your students have a positive experience.

in addition to that, consider the reputation and track record of the platform. Look for reviews and testimonials from other course creators to gauge their experiences with the platform. Choosing a platform with a strong reputation can provide peace of mind and confidence in your decision.

Create Engaging Content:

Creating engaging content for online courses is crucial for attracting and retaining students. To start, it's important to understand your target audience and their learning preferences. Conducting research or surveys can help you gather insights into what type of content will resonate with your audience. Once you have a clear understanding of your audience, you can tailor your content to meet their needs and preferences.

One effective strategy for creating engaging content is to incorporate multimedia elements such as videos, infographics, and interactive quizzes. These elements can help break up the monotony of text-based content and keep students engaged. Additionally, using real-life examples and case studies can make the content more relatable and practical for students, increasing their engagement and understanding of the material.

Another key aspect of creating engaging content is to make it interactive. Including activities, discussions, and assignments can encourage students to actively participate in the learning process. This not only keeps them engaged but also helps reinforce their understanding of the material. Furthermore, providing regular feedback and opportunities for reflection can enhance the learning experience and keep students motivated.

In addition to multimedia and interactive elements, storytelling can be a powerful tool for creating engaging content. Sharing personal anecdotes, success stories, or even failures can help create an emotional connection with students and make the content more memorable. This can also help illustrate key concepts in a more compelling and relatable way.

Furthermore, it's important to keep the content visually appealing and easy to navigate. Using a clean and intuitive layout, incorporating visuals, and organizing the content into digestible chunks can make it more engaging and accessible for students. Additionally, using a variety of fonts, colours, and formatting can help emphasize key points and maintain visual interest.

Moreover, incorporating gamification elements into the content can make the learning experience more enjoyable and engaging. This can include adding badges, points, or leader-boards to encourage healthy competition and motivate students to stay engaged with the material. Gamification can also make the learning process more interactive and immersive, increasing student retention and motivation.

Furthermore, creating a sense of community within the online course can enhance engagement. Encouraging discussions, group projects, and peer collaboration can foster a supportive learning environment and keep students connected and motivated. Additionally, providing opportunities for networking and mentorship can further enhance the sense of community and engagement within the course.

It's also important to continuously update and refresh the content to keep it relevant and engaging. Staying current with industry trends, incorporating new examples or case studies, and seeking feedback from students can help ensure that the content remains fresh and compelling. Additionally, offering regular updates or bonus materials can incentivize students to stay engaged and continue their learning journey.

Creating engaging content also involves leveraging social media and other online platforms to promote the course and connect with potential students. Sharing valuable insights, teasers of the course content, and success stories can generate interest and excitement around the course. Engaging with the audience through live Q&A sessions, webinars, or social media posts can also help build a community around the course and attract more students.

Set the Price of Your Online Course:

Setting the price for your online course is a crucial decision that can significantly impact the success of your business. There are several factors to consider when determining the right price point for your course. First and foremost, it's important to understand the value that your course provides to your target audience. Consider the knowledge and skills that participants will gain from your course and how it can positively impact their lives or careers. This will help you gauge the perceived value of your course and justify the price you set.

Another important factor to consider is the level of competition in your niche. Research other similar courses in the market and analyze their pricing strategies. This will give you an idea of the price range that your potential customers are willing to pay for online courses in your industry. It's important to strike a balance between offering competitive pricing and ensuring that you are adequately compensated for the time and effort you put into creating the course.

Additionally, consider the cost of production and delivery of your course. This includes expenses such as content creation, platform fees, marketing, and customer support. It's important to factor in these costs when setting your price to ensure that you are able to cover your expenses and generate a profit.

Furthermore, take into account the perceived quality of your course. If you have invested in high-quality production, expert instructors, or exclusive content, you can justify a higher price point for your course. On the other hand, if your course is more basic or introductory, it may be more appropriate to set a lower price to attract a wider audience.

It's also important to consider the pricing model that best suits your target audience and business goals. You can opt for a one-time payment, subscription-based model, or tiered pricing with different levels of access. Each model has its own advantages and it's important to choose one that aligns with your audience's preferences and purchasing behavior.

Moreover, consider offering discounts or promotions to attract new customers or retain existing ones. This can help generate initial interest in your course and incentivize potential customers to make a purchase. However, be mindful of devaluing your course by offering discounts too frequently or excessively.

Another important aspect to consider is the perceived value of your course in relation to the price. It's essential to effectively communicate the benefits and outcomes of your course to potential customers. This can be achieved through compelling marketing materials, testimonials, and a clear outline of what participants can expect to learn and achieve by enrolling in your course.

Lastly, it's crucial to continuously monitor and adjust your pricing strategy based on market trends, customer feedback, and the performance of your course. Regularly evaluate the impact of your pricing on sales and revenue, and be open to making changes to optimize your pricing strategy for long-term success.

In conclusion, setting the price for your online course requires careful consideration of various factors such as perceived value, competition, production costs, quality, pricing model, promotions, communication, and ongoing evaluation. By taking these factors into account and making informed decisions, you can set a price that not only reflects the value of your course but also attracts and retains customers while ensuring profitability for your business.

Market Your Online Course:

Marketing your online course is essential to reaching your target audience and generating sales. There are several strategies you can use to effectively market and sell your online course. First, it's important to identify your target audience and understand their needs and preferences. This will help you tailor your marketing efforts to appeal to potential students who are most likely to be interested in your course.

One effective way to market your online course is to create a compelling sales page that highlights the benefits of taking your course. This could include testimonials from previous students, a detailed outline of the course content, and any bonuses or additional resources that students will receive upon enrolling. You can also use persuasive copywriting to emphasize the value of your course and encourage visitors to take action.

In addition to creating a sales page, you can also use content marketing to promote your online course. This could involve creating blog posts, videos, or other types of content that provide valuable information related to the topic of your course. By sharing helpful and relevant content, you can establish yourself as an authority in your niche and attract potential students who are interested in learning more about the subject.

Another effective marketing strategy for selling online courses is to leverage the power of social media. You can use platforms like Facebook, Instagram, and LinkedIn to connect with potential students and promote your course. This could involve sharing engaging content, running targeted ads, or participating in relevant groups and communities where your target audience is active.

In addition to social media, email marketing can also be a powerful tool for promoting your online course. By building an email list of interested prospects, you can send targeted messages that highlight the benefits of your course and encourage recipients to enrol. You can also use email marketing to provide valuable content and build relationships with potential students over time.

Furthermore, collaborating with influencers or other experts in your niche can help you reach a wider audience and build credibility for your online course. By partnering with individuals who have a strong following or expertise in your subject area, you can tap into their network and leverage their influence to promote your course to a larger audience.

Additionally, offering a free webinar or workshop related to the topic of your online course can be an effective way to attract potential students and generate interest in your offering. By providing valuable information and insights during the webinar, you can demonstrate your expertise and build trust with attendees, making them more likely to enrol in your course.

Furthermore, implementing a referral program can help you leverage the power of word-of-mouth marketing to promote your online course. By incentivizing current students or satisfied customers to refer their friends and colleagues to your course, you can tap into their networks and generate new leads and sales for your offering.

Note that, you should not don't underestimate the power of search engine optimization (SEO) for promoting your online course. By optimizing your website and content for relevant keywords related to your course topic, you can improve your visibility in search engine results and attract organic traffic from individuals who are actively searching for information on the subject.

Offer Free Content:

When developing and selling online courses, offering free content can be a powerful strategy to attract potential students and build trust in your expertise. There are several ways to offer free content that can help you reach a wider audience and ultimately drive sales of your paid courses.

One effective approach is to create a free mini-course that provides a taste of the valuable content and insights that students can expect from your full courses. This mini-course can be delivered via email or through a dedicated section of your website, and it should be designed to showcase your expertise and the unique value you offer as an instructor. By providing a high-quality free mini-course, you can demonstrate the value of your paid courses and entice students to enrol in the complete program.

Another way to offer free content is through webinars and live events. Hosting free webinars on topics related to your course content can help you connect with potential students and showcase your knowledge in a live, interactive setting. This can be a powerful way to engage with your audience, answer their questions, and demonstrate the value of your expertise. Additionally, offering free live events such as workshops or Q&A sessions can further establish your credibility and attract students to your paid courses.

In addition to creating standalone free content, you can also offer free previews of your paid courses to give potential students a glimpse of what they can expect. This might include providing access to a few lessons or modules from your full course, allowing students to experience the quality and depth of your content before making a purchase. By offering these free previews, you can build interest in your paid courses and encourage students to take the next step toward enrolment.

Furthermore, creating and sharing valuable free resources such as eBooks, guides, or templates related to your course topic can be an effective way to attract potential students. By providing these resources for free, you can demonstrate your expertise and provide immediate value to your audience. This can help build trust and establish you as a knowledgeable authority in your field, making it more likely that students will consider enrolling in your paid courses.

Another approach to offering free content is through content marketing, such as blogging or creating videos on platforms like YouTube. By consistently sharing high-quality content related to your course topic, you can attract an audience of potential students who are interested in learning more from you. This content can serve as a valuable resource for your audience while also promoting your paid courses and driving traffic to your sales pages.

Additionally, leveraging social media platforms to offer free content can be an effective way to reach a wider audience and generate interest in your courses. This might include sharing valuable tips, insights, or short lessons related to your course topic on platforms like Facebook, Instagram, or LinkedIn. By providing valuable content for free on social media, you can engage with potential students and encourage them to explore your paid course offerings.

Moreover, collaborating with other experts in your field to create joint free content can help you expand your reach and attract new students. This might involve co-hosting webinars, creating co-authored blog posts, or participating in joint podcast episodes. By partnering with other experts, you can leverage each other's audiences and provide valuable free content that showcases the expertise and unique perspectives of both instructors.

More so, offering free trials of your paid courses can be an effective way to give potential students a hands-on experience with your content. By providing temporary access to the full course or selected modules, students can explore the value and benefits of your program before making a commitment. This can help alleviate any hesitation or uncertainty they may have about enrolling in your paid courses and ultimately lead to more conversions.

Engaging with your audience through email marketing can be a powerful way to offer free content and nurture relationships with potential students. By regularly sending valuable insights, tips, and resources related to your course topic via email, you can provide ongoing value to your audience while also promoting your paid courses. This approach can help you stay top-of-mind with potential students and build trust over time, increasing the likelihood that they will enrol in your courses.

Offering free content is an essential strategy for developing and selling online courses. By providing valuable resources, insights, and experiences for free, you can attract a wider audience, build trust in your expertise, and ultimately drive sales of your paid courses. Whether through mini-courses, webinars, free previews, valuable resources, content marketing, social media, collaborations, free trials, or email marketing, there are numerous effective ways to offer free content that can help you succeed in the online course market.

Create a Sales Page:

When creating a sales page for your online course, it's important to start by clearly identifying your target audience. Understanding who your course is for will help you tailor your sales page to speak directly to their needs and pain points. This will make it more likely that they will see the value in your course and be compelled to purchase it.

Once you have a clear understanding of your target audience, you can begin to craft your sales page messaging. Your headline should be attention-grabbing and clearly communicate the main benefit of your course. Use language that resonates with your audience and speaks to the transformation they will experience by taking your course.

In addition to a compelling headline, it's important to include a strong value proposition on your sales page. This should clearly outline what sets your course apart from others on the market and why it's worth the investment. Use specific examples and results to demonstrate the value of your course.

Another key element of a successful sales page is social proof. Including testimonials from past students or clients can help build trust and credibility with potential customers. Consider including before-and-after stories or case studies that demonstrate the results people have achieved by taking your course.

In addition to testimonials, it can be helpful to include a section on your sales page that addresses common objections or concerns that potential customers may have. Anticipating and addressing these objections can help alleviate any doubts and make it easier for people to make the decision to purchase your course.

When it comes to the design of your sales page, simplicity is key. Avoid clutter and distractions, and focus on guiding visitors through a clear and compelling sales message. Use visuals strategically to support your messaging and make the page visually appealing.

In terms of the actual sales process, it's important to make it as easy as possible for people to purchase your course. This means having a clear call-to-action that stands out on the page and leads visitors to a simple and straightforward purchasing process.

Finally, it's important to test and iterate on your sales page to ensure that it's effectively converting visitors into customers. Use A/B testing to experiment with different elements of your sales page, such as headlines, calls-to-action, and pricing, and use the data to continually optimize and improve your sales page's performance.

Creating an effective sales page for your online course involves understanding your audience, crafting compelling messaging, including social proof, addressing objections, designing a visually appealing page, simplifying the purchasing process, and testing and iterating for continual improvement. By following these steps, you can create a sales page that effectively communicates the value of your course and persuades visitors to become customers.

Provide Support and Engagement:

To provide support and engagement in developing and selling your online courses, it's important to first establish a strong foundation for your course. This means conducting thorough research to understand your target audience and their needs, as well as identifying the most effective teaching methods and resources to create a high-quality course. Once you have a clear understanding of your course content and structure, you can begin to develop engaging and interactive materials that will keep your students motivated and eager to learn.

In addition to creating compelling course content, it's essential to provide ongoing support and engagement for your students throughout the duration of the course. This can be achieved through regular communication and feedback, such as providing timely responses to student inquiries and offering constructive criticism on their work. By creating an open and supportive learning environment, you can foster a sense of community among your students and encourage them to actively participate in the course.

Another key aspect of providing support and engagement in developing and selling your online courses is to leverage various online platforms and tools to enhance the learning experience. For example, you can utilize discussion forums, live webinars, and interactive quizzes to keep your students engaged and motivated. Additionally, incorporating multimedia elements such as videos, podcasts, and infographics can help to make the course content more dynamic and appealing to a wider audience.

Furthermore, it's important to offer personalized support to address the individual needs of your students. This can involve providing one-on-one coaching sessions, personalized feedback on assignments, and tailored resources to help students overcome any challenges they may face. By demonstrating a genuine interest in the success of your students, you can build trust and loyalty, which can lead to positive word-of-mouth referrals and repeat business.

In order to effectively sell your online courses, it's crucial to develop a comprehensive marketing strategy that highlights the unique value proposition of your courses. This may involve creating compelling sales pages, utilizing social media and email marketing campaigns, and collaborating with influencers or affiliates to reach a wider audience. By effectively promoting your courses and communicating their benefits, you can generate interest and drive sales.

Moreover, offering incentives such as early-bird discounts, bonus materials, or money-back guarantees can help to entice potential students and increase conversion rates. Additionally, providing transparent pricing and flexible payment options can make your courses more accessible and appealing to a broader range of learners.

To maximize the success of your online courses, it's essential to continuously evaluate and improve your offerings based on student feedback and market trends. This may involve conducting surveys, analyzing course performance metrics, and staying informed about industry developments to ensure that your courses remain relevant and competitive. By staying agile and responsive to the needs of your audience, you can adapt your courses to meet evolving demands and maintain a loyal customer base.

Please note that providing support and engagement in developing and selling your online courses requires a multifaceted approach that prioritizes high-quality content, ongoing communication, personalized support, effective marketing, and continuous improvement. By focusing on these key areas, you can create a compelling learning experience for your students and drive the success of your online courses.

Analyze Performance:

To analyze your performance in developing and selling your online courses, it is important to first establish clear and measurable goals. These goals could include the number of courses you aim to develop within a certain time frame, the revenue you aim to generate from course sales, or the number of students you aim to enrol in your courses. Once you have established your goals, you can begin to analyze your performance by tracking key metrics and indicators.

One important aspect to consider when analyzing your performance in developing and selling online courses is the quality of the content you are offering. This can be measured by looking at student feedback and reviews, as well as tracking metrics such as completion rates and engagement levels. By analyzing this data, you can identify areas for improvement and make necessary adjustments to your course content.

Another important aspect to consider is the effectiveness of your marketing and sales strategies. This can be analyzed by tracking metrics such as conversion rates, click-through rates, and customer acquisition costs. By analyzing this data, you can identify which marketing channels are most effective for promoting your courses, as well as which sales strategies are most successful in converting leads into paying customers.

In addition to analyzing the quality of your content and the effectiveness of your marketing and sales strategies, it is also important to analyze the overall financial performance of your online courses. This includes tracking metrics such as revenue, profit margins, and return on investment. By analyzing this data, you can assess the financial viability of your courses and make informed decisions about pricing, cost management, and resource allocation.

It is important to analyze the engagement and satisfaction levels of your students. This can be done through surveys, feedback forms, and by tracking metrics such as course completion rates and student retention rates. By analyzing this data, you can gain valuable insights into the needs and preferences of your target audience, which can help inform future course development and marketing strategies.

Moreover, it is crucial to analyze the competitive landscape and industry trends to understand how your courses are performing relative to others in the market. This can be done by conducting market research, monitoring competitor activity, and staying informed about industry developments. By analyzing this data, you can identify opportunities for differentiation and innovation, as well as potential threats to your business.

Additionally, it is important to analyze the efficiency of your operations and processes in developing and selling online courses. This can be done by tracking metrics such as production costs, time-to-market, and customer support response times. By analyzing this data, you can identify areas for optimization and streamlining, which can help improve the overall performance and profitability of your courses.

Another important aspect to consider when analyzing your performance is the effectiveness of your customer support and service. This can be measured by tracking metrics such as customer satisfaction scores, response times to inquiries, and resolution rates for issues or complaints. By analyzing this data, you can identify areas for improvement in your customer support processes and ensure a positive experience for your students.

It is important to analyze the impact of external factors such as changes in technology, regulations, or market conditions on the performance of your online courses. By staying informed about these external factors and analyzing their impact on your business, you can adapt your strategies and operations accordingly to maintain a competitive edge in the market.

Iterate and Improve:

Developing and selling online courses is a continuous process that requires constant iteration and improvement. The first step in this process is to thoroughly research your target audience and their needs. Understanding the demographics, learning preferences, and pain points of your potential students will help you create courses that are tailored to their specific needs. This research will also help you identify gaps in the market that you can fill with your course offerings. By continuously gathering feedback from your students and potential customers, you can refine your courses to better meet their needs.

Once you have a clear understanding of your target audience, it's important to focus on creating high-quality content. This includes not only the course material itself, but also the delivery method. Utilize a variety of media, such as videos, interactive quizzes, and downloadable resources, to keep your students engaged and enhance their learning experience. Additionally, regularly updating and improving your course content based on industry trends and feedback will help you stay competitive in the market.

In order to effectively sell your online courses, it's essential to have a strong marketing strategy in place. This involves creating compelling sales copy, utilizing social media and email marketing, and leveraging partnerships with influencers or other businesses in your industry. By continuously analyzing the performance of your marketing efforts and making adjustments as needed, you can maximize your course sales and reach a wider audience.

In addition to marketing, providing exceptional customer support is crucial for the success of your online courses. This includes promptly addressing any technical issues that students may encounter, as well as being responsive to their questions and concerns. By consistently delivering outstanding customer service, you can build a loyal student base and generate positive word-of-mouth referrals.

Another important aspect of iterating and improving in developing and selling online courses is to stay updated on industry best practices and technological advancements. This involves regularly attending relevant conferences and workshops, as well as networking with other professionals in the e-learning space. By staying informed about the latest trends and tools, you can ensure that your courses remain relevant and competitive in the market.

Furthermore, seeking out partnerships with other businesses or organizations can provide valuable opportunities for growth and exposure. This could involve collaborating with industry experts to co-create courses, or partnering with companies to offer your courses as part of their employee training programs. By continuously seeking out strategic partnerships, you can expand your reach and attract new students to your courses.

Most importantly, it's important to regularly analyze the performance of your online courses in terms of sales, student engagement, and customer satisfaction. This involves tracking key metrics such as conversion rates, course completion rates, and student feedback. By consistently reviewing this data and identifying areas for improvement, you can make informed decisions about how to iterate and enhance your courses for better results.

By following these steps, you can start making money by developing and selling online courses.

Chapter 8
Writing and Publishing an E-book:

An e-book, short for electronic book, is a digital version of a traditional printed book that can be read on a computer or any handheld device equipped with an e-reader application. E-books can be accessed and downloaded from the internet, making them easily accessible to readers around the world. Unlike physical books, e-books do not require paper, ink, or other materials for production, making them an environmentally friendly alternative. E-books can also incorporate multimedia elements such as images, videos, and hyperlinks, providing an interactive reading experience for users. Additionally, e-books can be easily updated and revised, ensuring that the content remains current and relevant.

One of the key features of e-books is their portability and convenience. With an e-reader or a smartphone, readers can carry an entire library of e-books with them wherever they go, eliminating the need to lug around heavy physical books. This convenience makes e-books an ideal choice for travelers, students, and anyone who enjoys reading on the go. Furthermore, e-books often offer adjustable font sizes and customizable settings, allowing readers to personalize their reading experience to suit their preferences.

E-books have also revolutionized the publishing industry by providing a platform for independent authors to self-publish their work without the need for a traditional publishing house. This has led to a proliferation of new voices and diverse perspectives in the literary world. Additionally, e-books have made it easier for authors to reach a global audience, as they can distribute their work digitally without the constraints of physical distribution and inventory management. This has democratized the publishing process and empowered writers to share their stories with readers worldwide.

Another benefit of e-books is their searchability and accessibility features. Readers can easily search for specific keywords or phrases within an e-book, making it simple to locate relevant information quickly. Additionally, e-books can be equipped with features such as text-to-speech functionality and audio narration, making them accessible to individuals with visual impairments or learning disabilities. This inclusivity ensures that e-books can be enjoyed by a wide range of audiences, regardless of their individual needs or preferences.

E-books also offer cost savings for both readers and publishers. Without the overhead costs associated with printing, storing, and distributing physical books, e-books are often priced lower than their printed counterparts, making them a more affordable option for consumers. This cost-effectiveness also extends to publishers, who can produce and distribute e-books at a fraction of the cost of traditional printing methods. As a result, e-books have opened up new opportunities for smaller publishers and independent authors to enter the market and compete with larger publishing houses.

The evolution of e-books has also given rise to new formats and distribution models, such as subscription services and digital libraries. These platforms offer readers access to a vast collection of e-books for a flat monthly fee, providing an affordable and convenient way to discover new titles and authors. Furthermore, e-books have facilitated the development of enhanced e-book editions that incorporate interactive features, multimedia content, and immersive storytelling experiences. These innovations have expanded the possibilities of digital reading and have redefined the way stories are told and consumed in the digital age.

E-books have transformed the way we read, write, and publish literature by offering a versatile, accessible, and sustainable alternative to traditional printed books. With their portability, affordability, and interactive capabilities, e-books have become an integral part of contemporary reading culture. As technology continues to advance, e-books will undoubtedly continue to evolve and innovate, shaping the future of storytelling and literary consumption for generations to come.

Making money by writing and publishing e-books involves creating and selling digital books to readers through various online platforms. Certainly! How to make money writing and selling e-books is a topic that encompasses various aspects of self-publishing and generating income through digital books.

Writing and publishing an e-book can be a lucrative way to make money. To start, you'll need to choose a topic that you are knowledgeable and passionate about. This will make the writing process more enjoyable and ensure that you produce high-quality content. Once you have a topic in mind, it's important to conduct thorough research to ensure that your e-book provides valuable and accurate information. This will help establish your credibility as an author and increase the likelihood of attracting readers.

After completing the writing process, it's time to focus on the publishing and marketing aspects of your e-book. There are various platforms available for self-publishing, such as Amazon Kindle Direct Publishing and Smashwords, which allow you to easily upload and sell your e-book online. It's important to carefully consider pricing strategies and promotional efforts to maximize sales. Utilizing social media, email marketing, and other digital channels can help increase visibility and attract potential readers.

In addition to direct sales, consider exploring other revenue streams such as offering related products or services, creating a series of e-books, or licensing your content for use in other publications. By diversifying your income sources, you can maximize the earning potential of your e-book. It's also important to continuously engage with your audience by seeking feedback, responding to inquiries, and providing updates or additional content to maintain reader interest and loyalty.

Another way to make money from your e-book is by leveraging affiliate marketing. You can strategically incorporate affiliate links within your e-book to promote relevant products or services that align with your content. When readers make a purchase through these links, you can earn a commission, providing an additional source of passive income. It's important to disclose any affiliate relationships transparently and ethically to maintain trust with your audience.

Furthermore, consider exploring opportunities for collaboration or partnerships with other authors or influencers in your niche. By cross-promoting each other's e-books or co-authoring a publication, you can expand your reach and attract new readers. Collaborative efforts can also provide valuable insights and support, ultimately contributing to the success and profitability of your e-book.

As with any business venture, it's essential to continuously monitor and analyze the performance of your e-book to identify areas for improvement and optimization. By tracking sales data, reader engagement metrics, and market trends, you can make informed decisions to enhance the profitability of your e-book. This may involve updating content, adjusting pricing strategies, or exploring new marketing tactics to adapt to changing consumer preferences and market dynamics.

Making money through writing and publishing an e-book requires a strategic approach that encompasses various stages from content creation to distribution and monetization. By leveraging your expertise, conducting thorough research, implementing effective marketing strategies, exploring diverse revenue streams, and continuously refining your approach based on performance insights, you can maximize the earning potential of your e-book. With dedication, creativity, and persistence, writing and publishing an e-book can be a rewarding endeavor both financially and professionally.

If you really want to publish profitable, high-quality content with appealing cover with competitive price, use Amazon kindle Direct Publication. There is money upfront to pay in joining amazon and the bigger amazon traffic will be enjoyed by you as you use all amazon tools at achieve your desired success.

To make money by writing and publishing an eBook, follow these steps:

Choose a Topic:

When choosing a niche for writing and publishing an e-book, it's important to consider your own interests and expertise. Think about what topics you are passionate about and have a deep knowledge of. This will not only make the writing process more enjoyable for you, but it will also ensure that you are providing valuable and credible information to your readers. Consider your hobbies, professional experience, or personal interests that you can leverage into a niche for your e-book.

Another important factor to consider when choosing a niche for your e-book is the market demand. Research the current trends and popular topics within the e-book industry to identify potential niches that have a high demand. Look for topics that have a large audience and are consistently sought after by readers. This will increase the likelihood of your e-book being successful and reaching a wide audience.

It's also essential to consider the competition within your chosen niche. While it's important to select a niche with high demand, it's equally important to assess the level of competition within that niche. Look for a niche where you can offer a unique perspective or provide something different from what is already available in the market. This will help you stand out from the competition and attract readers who are looking for fresh and innovative content.

Consider the profitability of your chosen niche. While passion and expertise are important, it's also crucial to consider the potential financial return of your e-book. Research the pricing and sales trends within your chosen niche to determine if it has the potential to generate a significant income. Look for niches where readers are willing to invest in valuable content and where there is a proven track record of successful e-books generating substantial revenue.

When choosing a niche for your e-book, it's important to consider the long-term potential of the topic. Look for niches that have longevity and will remain relevant over time. Avoid topics that are too trendy or short-lived, as this may limit the shelf life of your e-book. Instead, focus on evergreen topics or subjects that have enduring appeal and will continue to be relevant to readers in the future.

Consider the target audience for your e-book when choosing a niche. Think about who your ideal readers are and what kind of content would resonate with them. Consider their demographics, interests, and preferences to tailor your niche to meet their needs. Understanding your target audience will help you create content that is highly relevant and valuable to them, increasing the likelihood of your e-book's success.

Lastly, consider the potential for expansion within your chosen niche. Look for niches that offer opportunities for future growth and development. Consider how you can create additional e-books or related products within the same niche to build a comprehensive brand and attract repeat customers. Choosing a niche with room for expansion will allow you to build a sustainable and profitable writing and publishing business in the long run.

Research Your Audience:

When it comes to writing and publishing an e-book, it's crucial to thoroughly research your audience to ensure that your content resonates with them. One effective way to research your audience is by conducting surveys and interviews. By asking targeted questions, you can gain valuable insights into the preferences, interests, and needs of your potential readers. This information can then be used to tailor your e-book content to better meet the expectations of your audience.

Another useful method for researching your audience is by analyzing data from social media and online forums. By monitoring discussions and trends related to your e-book topic, you can gain a deeper understanding of the issues that are important to your audience. This can help you identify common pain points and interests, which can then be addressed in your e-book to make it more relevant and valuable to your readers.

In addition to surveys and social media analysis, it's important to conduct keyword research to understand what terms and phrases your audience is using to search for information related to your e-book topic. By identifying popular keywords, you can optimize your e-book content to make it more discoverable to your target audience. This can help increase the visibility of your e-book and attract more potential readers.

Furthermore, researching your audience also involves studying the competition. By analyzing similar e-books in your niche, you can gain insights into what has worked well for other authors and identify gaps or opportunities for differentiation. This can help you refine your e-book concept and positioning to better appeal to your target audience.

Moreover, it's essential to consider the demographic characteristics of your audience, such as age, gender, location, and education level. Understanding these factors can help you create content that is tailored to the specific needs and preferences of your target readers. For example, if your e-book is targeted towards young adults, you may want to use language and references that resonate with this demographic.

Another important aspect of researching your audience has to do with understanding their buying behaviour and preferences. By analyzing purchasing patterns and consumer behaviour within your target market, you can gain valuable insights into how to position and promote your e-book effectively. This can help you develop a marketing strategy that resonates with your audience and maximizes the potential for sales.

Please note that it is important to engage with your audience directly through social media, email lists, and other channels. By actively listening to feedback and engaging in conversations with your potential readers, you can gain valuable insights into their preferences and expectations. This direct interaction can provide invaluable feedback that can inform the content and marketing strategies for your e-book.

Plan Your Content:

When planning to write and publish an e-book, it's important to start with a clear understanding of your target audience and their needs. Take the time to research and identify the specific topics and themes that will resonate with your readers. Consider conducting surveys or interviews to gather insights into the interests and preferences of your potential readers. By understanding your audience, you can tailor your content to meet their needs and ensure that your e-book is relevant and valuable to them.

After identifying your target audience, it's essential to create a detailed outline for your e-book. This outline should include a clear structure for your content, including chapters, sections, and subtopics. By creating a roadmap for your e-book, you can ensure that your content flows logically and effectively communicates your key messages. Additionally, an outline can help you stay focused and organized as you write, making the process more efficient and productive.

Once you have a solid outline in place, it's time to start creating the actual content for your e-book. When writing, it's important to maintain a consistent tone and style throughout the book. Whether you choose to be conversational, authoritative, or humorous, it's crucial to establish a voice that resonates with your target audience. Additionally, be sure to include compelling stories, examples, and case studies to illustrate your key points and make your content more engaging and relatable.

As you write, it's important to keep in mind the overall goal of your e-book. Are you seeking to educate, entertain, inspire, or persuade your readers? By clarifying your objectives, you can ensure that your content is aligned with your desired outcomes. Additionally, consider incorporating calls to action throughout your e-book to encourage readers to take the next steps, whether it's signing up for a newsletter, visiting your website, or purchasing a product or service.

In addition to creating compelling written content, consider incorporating visual elements into your e-book to enhance the reader experience. This could include photos, illustrations, infographics, or charts that help illustrate key concepts and break up the text. Visuals can make your e-book more visually appealing and easier to digest, particularly for readers who are more visually oriented. Just be sure to ensure that any visuals you use are high quality and relevant to your content.

Once you've completed the writing process, it's important to review and edit your e-book thoroughly. This may involve revising the content for clarity and conciseness, checking for grammatical and spelling errors, and ensuring that the overall flow and structure of the e-book are cohesive. Consider enlisting the help of a professional editor or asking trusted colleagues or beta readers to provide feedback on your e-book before finalizing it for publication.

When it comes to the time to publish your e-book, consider the various platforms and distribution channels available to you. Whether you choose to self-publish through platforms like Amazon Kindle Direct Publishing or work with a traditional publisher, it's important to consider the best approach for reaching your target audience. Additionally, think about how you will market and promote your e-book to generate interest and drive sales. This may involve leveraging social media, email marketing, content marketing, or other promotional tactics to raise awareness and attract readers to your e-book.

Write Compelling Content:

Writing compelling content for an e-book involves several key elements that can make your work stand out and resonate with your audience. First and foremost, it's essential to start with a clear understanding of your target audience. Knowing who you are writing for will help you tailor your content to their specific needs, interests, and pain points. This will enable you to create content that is relevant and valuable to your readers, increasing the likelihood of engagement and satisfaction.

Another crucial aspect of writing compelling e-book content is to establish a strong and captivating narrative. Whether you are writing fiction or non-fiction, storytelling is a powerful tool that can draw readers in and keep them engaged throughout the entire book. By developing well-rounded characters, creating a compelling plot, and using descriptive language, you can transport your readers into the world of your e-book and make them emotionally invested in the content.

In addition to storytelling, incorporating visual elements can also enhance the appeal of your e-book. Utilizing high-quality images, infographics, charts, and other visual aids can break up the text and make the content more visually appealing and easier to digest. Visual elements can also help reinforce key points, provide additional context, and create a more immersive reading experience for your audience.

Furthermore, it's important to ensure that your e-book is well-researched and provides valuable insights or information to your readers. Whether you are writing a how-to guide, a self-help book, or a work of fiction, conducting thorough research and providing accurate and reliable information will add credibility to your content. This can help establish you as an authority in your niche and build trust with your readers, increasing the likelihood of them recommending your e-book to others.

Moreover, writing in a clear and concise manner is essential for creating compelling e-book content. Avoiding unnecessary jargon, using simple language, and organizing your ideas in a logical and coherent manner will make your content more accessible and engaging for a wider audience. Additionally, using a conversational tone can make your writing feel more relatable and inviting, allowing readers to connect with the content on a more personal level.

Furthermore, incorporating interactive elements into your e-book can also enhance reader engagement. This can include interactive quizzes, polls, or links to additional resources that provide readers with a more immersive and interactive reading experience. By encouraging reader participation and providing opportunities for them to actively engage with the content, you can create a more memorable and impactful reading experience.

When writing compelling contents it is important to pay attention to the formatting and design of your e-book. Ensuring that the layout is visually appealing, the text is easy to read, and the overall design is cohesive and professional will contribute to the overall appeal of your e-book. A well-designed e-book will not only enhance the reading experience but also reflect positively on the quality and value of the content itself.

Edit and Proofread:

Editing and proofreading are crucial steps in the process of writing and publishing an e-book. These steps ensure that the final product is polished, professional, and free of errors. To begin, start by reviewing the content for clarity, coherence, and flow. Look for any inconsistencies in the plot, characters, or timeline. It's important to make sure that the story or information is presented in a logical and engaging manner. Additionally, check for any grammatical errors, spelling mistakes, or punctuation issues. This includes verifying that the text adheres to the appropriate style guide, whether it's APA, MLA, Chicago, or another standard.

After reviewing the content, it's time to focus on the structure and formatting of the e-book. This includes checking for proper headings, subheadings, and chapter organization. Make sure that the table of contents is accurate and that all page numbers correspond correctly. It's also important to verify that any images, charts, or graphs are correctly labeled and positioned within the text. Additionally, ensure that the font type and size are consistent throughout the e-book. Pay attention to spacing, indents, and margins as well.

Once the content and structure have been thoroughly reviewed, it's important to proofread for any typographical errors or formatting issues. This includes checking for widows, orphans, and awkward line breaks. It's also crucial to verify that all hyperlinks are functioning properly and directing readers to the correct WebPages. This step is essential for ensuring a seamless reading experience for the audience. Lastly, take the time to review the e-book on different devices and platforms to ensure that it appears correctly across various mediums.

In addition to reviewing the e-book on a technical level, it's important to also consider the overall tone and voice of the writing. Make sure that the language is appropriate for the intended audience and that it effectively conveys the desired message. This includes checking for any instances of jargon, slang, or colloquialisms that may not resonate with all readers. It's also important to verify that the tone remains consistent throughout the e-book and aligns with the author's intended style.

Another important aspect of editing and proofreading an e-book is verifying any factual information presented within the text. This includes checking references, citations, and sources to ensure accuracy and credibility. It's important to verify that all statistics, quotes, and data are correctly attributed and supported by reliable sources. Additionally, make sure that any historical or scientific information presented is accurate and up-to-date. This step is crucial for maintaining the e-book's integrity and trustworthiness.

After completing the initial round of editing and proofreading, it's beneficial to seek feedback from beta readers or colleagues. This can provide valuable insights into areas that may need further improvement or clarification. Consider conducting a focus group or survey to gather feedback on the e-book's content, design, and overall impact. It's important to remain open to constructive criticism and be willing to make necessary revisions based on the feedback received.

Before publishing the e-book, it's essential to conduct a final review to ensure that all changes have been implemented successfully. This includes checking for any last-minute errors or issues that may have been overlooked during previous rounds of editing and proofreading. Consider enlisting the help of a professional editor or proofreader for a final review before releasing the e-book to the public. By following these steps and taking the time to thoroughly edit and proofread an e-book, authors can ensure that their final product is polished, professional, and ready to captivate audiences.

Design the eBook:

Designing an e-book involves careful consideration of various elements such as layout, writing style, file format compatibility, cover design, distribution strategy, marketing efforts, and technical optimization. By focusing on these key aspects, authors can create a well-designed e-book that engages readers, delivers valuable content, and reaches a wider audience in today's digital landscape.

Designing an e-book involves several key considerations to ensure a successful writing and publishing process. Firstly, it is important to carefully plan the structure and layout of the e-book. This includes determining the overall flow of the content, organizing chapters and sections, and creating a visually appealing design. The layout should be user-friendly and easy to navigate, with clear headings, subheadings, and an intuitive table of contents. Additionally, incorporating multimedia elements such as images, videos, and interactive features can enhance the e-book's overall design and engage readers.

In addition to the layout, it is crucial to focus on the writing style and content of the e-book. The writing should be clear, concise, and engaging, tailored to the target audience. It is important to carefully edit and proofread the content to ensure it is free of errors and flows smoothly. Furthermore, incorporating high-quality, relevant information and providing valuable insights can help establish the e-book as a credible and authoritative resource. Additionally, integrating interactive elements such as quizzes, surveys, or links to additional resources can further engage readers and enhance the overall user experience.

Another important aspect of designing an e-book is selecting the appropriate file format and ensuring compatibility across various devices and platforms. Choosing a file format that supports multimedia elements and is compatible with e-readers, tablets, and smartphones can ensure a seamless reading experience for users. Additionally, optimizing the e-book for different screen sizes and resolutions can help maintain the design integrity across various devices. Furthermore, considering accessibility features such as text-to-speech capabilities and adjustable font sizes can make the e-book more inclusive and user-friendly.

Moreover, designing an effective e-book involves creating an eye-catching cover and title that captures the essence of the content and entices potential readers. The cover design should be visually appealing, relevant to the topic, and reflective of the e-book's overall style. Additionally, crafting a compelling title and subtitle can help pique readers' interest and convey the value of the e-book's content. Furthermore, incorporating endorsements or testimonials on the cover can help establish credibility and build trust with potential readers.

Furthermore, it is essential to consider the distribution and marketing strategy when designing an e-book. This includes determining the most suitable platforms for publishing and distributing the e-book, such as online marketplaces, self-publishing platforms, or personal websites. Additionally, developing a marketing plan to promote the e-book through social media, email campaigns, and other digital channels can help increase visibility and attract a wider audience. Moreover, leveraging search engine optimization (SEO) techniques to optimize the e-book's visibility in online searches can enhance its discoverability and reach.

Additionally, it is important to consider the technical aspects of designing an e-book, such as file size optimization, metadata tagging, and digital rights management (DRM). Optimizing the file size can help reduce download times and minimize storage requirements for users. Furthermore, implementing metadata tagging with relevant keywords and descriptions can improve the e-book's discoverability and search engine ranking. Additionally, considering DRM solutions to protect the e-book's intellectual property rights and prevent unauthorized distribution can safeguard the author's work and ensure fair compensation for their efforts.

Choose a Publishing Platform:

Choosing the right publishing platform for your e-book is a crucial decision that can greatly impact the success of your writing and publishing journey. There are several factors to consider when selecting the best platform for your e-book, including the platform's reach, ease of use, royalty rates, marketing tools, and pricing options. It's important to thoroughly research and compare different platforms to find the one that best meets your needs and goals as an author.

One of the most important considerations when choosing a publishing platform for your e-book is the platform's reach and audience. You'll want to select a platform that has a large and diverse audience of readers who are interested in your genre or niche. Look for platforms that have a strong presence in the e-book market and offer opportunities for exposure to new readers through features like recommendation algorithms, promotional tools, and targeted marketing campaigns.

Ease of use is another critical factor to consider when choosing a publishing platform for your e-book. Look for platforms that offer user-friendly interfaces, intuitive publishing processes, and comprehensive support resources. The last thing you want is to struggle with a complicated or cumbersome publishing platform when you should be focusing on writing and promoting your e-book.

Royalty rates are an important consideration when choosing a publishing platform for your e-book. Different platforms offer different royalty rates, so it's important to compare and evaluate the potential earnings from each platform. Some platforms offer higher royalty rates but may have stricter pricing requirements or exclusivity agreements, while others may offer lower rates but provide more flexibility and control over pricing and distribution.

Marketing tools and support are essential considerations when selecting a publishing platform for your e-book. Look for platforms that offer robust marketing tools, promotional opportunities, and support resources to help you reach new readers and maximize the visibility of your e-book. Some platforms provide features like targeted advertising, author profiles, and email marketing tools to help you connect with your audience and build a loyal reader base.

Pricing options are another important factor to consider when choosing a publishing platform for your e-book. Look for platforms that offer flexible pricing options, such as the ability to set your own e-book prices, run promotional discounts, and participate in bundled sales or subscription programs. It's important to have control over the pricing and discounting of your e-book to maximize your earnings and appeal to different segments of your target audience.

Another crucial consideration when choosing a publishing platform for your e-book is the platform's terms of service and contractual agreements. Take the time to carefully review and understand the terms of service, distribution agreements, and any exclusivity requirements before committing to a publishing platform. You'll want to ensure that the platform's terms align with your goals and expectations as an author and that you retain the rights and control over your e-book.

Please note that considering the overall reputation and track record of the publishing platform when making your decision is very important. Look for platforms with a proven history of success in the e-book market, positive reviews from authors, and a strong commitment to supporting and promoting their authors' work. A reputable publishing platform can provide valuable credibility, visibility, and support for your e-book, helping you reach a wider audience and achieve greater success as an author.

Set a Price:

Setting the price for your e-book is a crucial decision that can greatly impact its success. One of the first things to consider when determining the price of your e-book is the quality of the content. If your e-book is well-researched, professionally edited, and provides valuable information to the reader, then you can justify a higher price point. On the other hand, if your e-book is shorter, less polished, or targeted towards a niche audience, then a lower price may be more appropriate. It's important to be honest with yourself about the quality of your e-book and to set a price that reflects its true value.

In addition to considering the quality of your e-book, it's also important to research and compare prices on other platforms. Take the time to look at similar e-books in your genre and see what they are priced at. This will give you a better understanding of what readers are willing to pay for e-books like yours. Keep in mind that pricing can vary greatly depending on the platform, so it's important to look at multiple sources such as Amazon, Barnes & Noble, and other e-book retailers. By doing this research, you can ensure that your e-book is competitively priced and positioned for success in the market.

Another important factor to consider when setting the price for your e-book is the value it provides to the reader. If your e-book offers unique insights, actionable advice, or solves a specific problem for the reader, then you can justify a higher price. Conversely, if your e-book is more of a casual read or entertainment-focused, then a lower price may be more appropriate. It's important to think about the value proposition of your e-book and how it will be perceived by potential readers. By aligning the price with the value it provides, you can increase the likelihood of attracting and retaining readers.

Furthermore, it's important to consider the length and depth of the content when setting the price for your e-book. Longer, more in-depth e-books typically command higher prices because they offer more value to the reader. Conversely, shorter e-books may be priced lower because they offer less content. It's important to strike a balance between providing enough value to justify the price and ensuring that the price is accessible to your target audience. Consider how much time and effort went into creating the content and use that as a guide for determining the price.

Moreover, it's important to take into account any additional resources or bonuses that come with the e-book when setting the price. For example, if your e-book includes access to a private online community, downloadable templates, or bonus chapters, then these additional resources can justify a higher price. On the other hand, if your e-book is a standalone product without any extras, then a lower price may be more appropriate. By considering the full package that you are offering to readers, you can create a pricing strategy that reflects the overall value of your e-book.

In addition to considering the quality of your e-book and checking prices from other platforms, it's also important to think about your long-term goals when setting the price. If your main objective is to maximize profits, then you may lean towards a higher price point. However, if your goal is to reach a wider audience and build a loyal readership, then a lower price may be more strategic. It's important to weigh these factors and consider how they align with your overall publishing and marketing strategy. By setting a price that aligns with your goals, you can set yourself up for success in the long run.

Finally, it's important to remain flexible with your pricing strategy and be open to adjusting the price based on feedback and performance. Once your e-book is live, pay attention to sales data, reader reviews, and any other relevant metrics to gauge how well it's performing in the market. If you find that the initial price is not resonating with readers or impacting sales, don't be afraid to experiment with different price points. By remaining open-minded and willing to make adjustments, you can optimize the pricing for your e-book and maximize its potential for success.

Market Your EBook:

Marketing an e-book is crucial to its success in the competitive world of digital publishing. To effectively market your e-book, you need to start by identifying your target audience and understanding their needs and preferences. This will help you tailor your marketing efforts to reach the right people and increase your chances of success. Once you have a clear understanding of your target audience, you can begin to develop a marketing strategy that will help you reach them. This may include creating a website or blog to promote your e-book, using social media to connect with potential readers, and reaching out to influencers in your niche to help spread the word about your book.

In addition to understanding your target audience, it's important to have a strong understanding of the competitive landscape in your niche. This will help you identify opportunities to differentiate your e-book from others in the market and develop a unique selling proposition that will appeal to potential readers. By understanding the strengths and weaknesses of your competitors, you can position your e-book in a way that highlights its unique value and makes it stand out from the crowd.

Once you have a clear understanding of your target audience and the competitive landscape, it's time to create a marketing plan for your e-book. This plan should outline the specific tactics and strategies you will use to promote your e-book, including the channels you will use to reach potential readers, the messaging you will use to communicate the value of your e-book, and the timeline for executing your marketing activities. By creating a detailed marketing plan, you can ensure that you are focused and organized in your efforts to promote your e-book.

One effective way to market your e-book is to leverage the power of content marketing. This involves creating high-quality, valuable content that is relevant to your target audience and using it to attract and engage potential readers. For example, you could write blog posts or articles related to the topic of your e-book, create videos or podcasts that provide valuable information to your target audience, or develop infographics or other visual content that helps communicate the key messages of your e-book. By creating and sharing valuable content, you can build trust and credibility with potential readers and increase awareness of your e-book.

Another important aspect of marketing your e-book is building a strong online presence. This includes creating a professional website or landing page for your e-book, optimizing it for search engines so that potential readers can find it easily, and using social media and other online channels to connect with potential readers. By building a strong online presence, you can increase the visibility of your e-book and make it easier for potential readers to discover and purchase it.

In addition to leveraging content marketing and building a strong online presence, it's important to consider other promotional tactics that can help you reach potential readers. For example, you could offer free sample chapters of your e-book to entice readers to purchase the full version, run promotions or discounts to generate interest and sales, or collaborate with other authors or influencers in your niche to cross-promote each other's work. By using a combination of promotional tactics, you can increase the visibility and appeal of your e-book and attract more readers.

It's important to continuously evaluate and refine your marketing efforts to ensure that they are effective in promoting your e-book. This may involve tracking key metrics such as website traffic, social media engagement, and e-book sales, soliciting feedback from readers and other stakeholders, and making adjustments to your marketing plan as needed. By continuously monitoring and improving your marketing efforts, you can maximize the success of your e-book and increase its impact in the market.

Offer Free Content:

Offering free content in writing and publishing an e-book can be a great way to attract readers and build a loyal following. One effective strategy is to offer a free sample of the e-book, such as the first chapter or a few select pages, to give potential readers a taste of what they can expect. This can entice them to purchase the full e-book if they enjoy the sample, and it also serves as a way to showcase your writing style and the value of your content. By providing valuable and engaging free content, you can demonstrate your expertise and build trust with your audience, making them more likely to invest in your full e-book or future publications.

Another approach to offering free content in writing and publishing an e-book is to create a companion guide or workbook that complements the e-book's content. This can provide additional value to readers and encourage them to engage more deeply with your material. For example, if your e-book is about personal finance, you could offer a free budgeting template or financial planning checklist as a downloadable resource. By providing practical tools and resources for free, you can enhance the overall experience for your readers and position yourself as a helpful and generous author.

In addition to offering free samples and companion materials, you can also create bonus content that is exclusively available to those who purchase the e-book. This could include access to a private online community or discussion forum where readers can connect with you and other fans of your work, as well as exclusive interviews, behind-the-scenes content, or additional chapters that expand on the e-book's themes. By offering valuable bonuses to those who support your work, you can incentivize purchases while still providing free content to attract new readers.

Furthermore, consider creating a series of free blog posts or articles that expand on the topics covered in your e-book. This can help you reach a wider audience and establish yourself as an authority in your niche. By sharing valuable insights and information for free, you can attract readers who may be interested in delving deeper into the subject matter by purchasing your e-book. Additionally, you can repurpose this free content by including it in your e-book's marketing materials, such as email newsletters, social media posts, and promotional videos, to further entice potential readers.

Moreover, consider offering a free mini-course or webinar that covers key concepts from your e-book in more detail. This can serve as an educational resource for your audience and provide a preview of the valuable content they can expect from your e-book. By delivering high-quality free content through a mini-course or webinar, you can demonstrate your expertise and build credibility with potential readers, making them more likely to invest in your full e-book to gain access to additional insights and knowledge.

Additionally, consider collaborating with other authors or experts in your field to create a free digital anthology or collection of essays that showcases diverse perspectives on the topics addressed in your e-book. This can help you reach new audiences and provide valuable content that complements your e-book while also introducing readers to other authors they may be interested in. By offering this collaborative anthology for free, you can attract readers who are curious about the subject matter and may be inclined to explore more by purchasing your e-book or other related publications.

In order to achieve more, consider offering a limited-time promotion where you make your e-book available for free download for a specific period. This can generate buzz and excitement around your work, attract new readers who may be hesitant to purchase without sampling the content first, and potentially lead to increased sales once the promotion ends. By strategically timing this free offer to coincide with relevant events or holidays, you can capitalize on increased interest and engagement from potential readers who are seeking valuable content at no cost.

Create a Sales Page:

Writing and publishing an e-book can be an exciting and rewarding endeavour, but in order to achieve success, it's crucial to create a compelling sales page that effectively promotes your work. A sales page is essentially a landing page that is designed to persuade potential readers to purchase your e-book. To create a sales page that converts, it's important to start by clearly defining your target audience and understanding their needs and desires. This will allow you to tailor your messaging and content to resonate with your ideal readers, increasing the likelihood of making a sale.

Once you have a clear understanding of your target audience, it's time to craft a compelling headline that grabs their attention and entices them to keep reading. Your headline should clearly communicate the value proposition of your e-book and highlight the benefits that readers will gain from purchasing and reading it. Additionally, incorporating persuasive language and emotional triggers can help to further engage potential buyers and encourage them to take action.

In addition to a captivating headline, it's essential to provide a detailed description of your e-book that highlights its unique selling points and addresses the specific pain points or challenges that your target audience may be facing. By clearly articulating the value and relevance of your e-book, you can effectively demonstrate why it's a must-read for your audience and differentiate it from other similar offerings in the market.

Another key component of a successful sales page is the inclusion of social proof, such as testimonials or reviews from satisfied readers or industry experts. Social proof serves to build credibility and trust with potential buyers, as it provides evidence that others have found value in your e-book and validates the claims you've made about its quality and impact. Including compelling testimonials can help to alleviate any doubts or scepticism that potential buyers may have and increase their confidence in making a purchase.

Furthermore, incorporating visually appealing graphics, such as high-quality images of your e-book cover or mock-ups of the content, can enhance the overall appeal of your sales page and capture the attention of potential buyers. Visual elements can help to break up the text and make the page more engaging, while also providing a tangible representation of your e-book that can further entice readers to make a purchase.

In addition to compelling visuals, it's important to include a clear call-to-action (CTA) that prompts visitors to take the next step, whether it's purchasing your e-book, signing up for a newsletter, or downloading a free sample chapter. Your CTA should be prominently displayed on the sales page and use persuasive language to encourage immediate action. By making it easy for visitors to take the desired action, you can increase the likelihood of converting them into paying customers.

Eventually, optimizing your sales page for search engines and ensuring that it is mobile-friendly can help to maximize its visibility and accessibility to potential buyers. By incorporating relevant keywords and meta tags, as well as ensuring that the page loads quickly and displays properly on mobile devices, you can improve its chances of ranking well in search results and provide a seamless browsing experience for visitors across different devices.

Engage with Your Audience:

Engaging with your audience in writing and publishing an e-book is essential for building a loyal readership and increasing the success of your book. One of the most effective ways to engage with your audience is by creating valuable and relevant content that addresses their needs and interests. This can be achieved through thorough research and understanding of your target audience's demographics, preferences, and behaviours. By tailoring your e-book content to meet the specific needs of your audience, you can establish a strong connection with them and increase their interest in your work.

In addition to creating valuable content, engaging with your audience also involves actively seeking their feedback and input throughout the writing and publishing process. This can be done through various channels such as social media, email newsletters, or online surveys. By soliciting feedback from your audience, you can gain valuable insights into their preferences, expectations, and concerns, which can help you refine your e-book content and make it more appealing to them. Moreover, involving your audience in the decision-making process can also make them feel valued and appreciated, leading to increased loyalty and support for your e-book.

Another effective way to engage with your audience in writing and publishing an e-book is by building a strong online presence through social media and other digital platforms. By actively participating in relevant online communities, sharing valuable content, and interacting with your audience, you can establish yourself as a credible and trustworthy author. This can help you build a loyal following and attract new readers to your e-book. Additionally, engaging with your audience through social media can also provide valuable opportunities for promoting your e-book, generating buzz, and increasing its visibility to potential readers.

Furthermore, engaging with your audience in writing and publishing an e-book also involves creating a sense of community and belonging among your readers. This can be achieved by fostering open communication, encouraging discussions, and creating opportunities for your audience to connect with each other. For example, you can create a dedicated online forum or community group where readers can share their thoughts, ask questions, and interact with each other. By facilitating these interactions, you can create a supportive and engaging environment that encourages readers to actively participate in discussions related to your e-book.

Moreover, engaging with your audience also involves providing ongoing support and value beyond the initial publication of your e-book. This can be done by offering additional resources, updates, or exclusive content to your readers through a dedicated email newsletter or membership program. By consistently providing value to your audience, you can maintain their interest in your work and encourage them to stay engaged with your future projects. Additionally, offering ongoing support and value can also help you build a loyal fan base that is more likely to recommend your e-book to others and support your future endeavours as an author.

Engaging with your audience in writing and publishing an e-book is crucial for building a loyal readership and increasing the success of your book. By creating valuable content, seeking feedback, building a strong online presence, fostering a sense of community, and providing ongoing support, you can establish a strong connection with your audience and increase their interest in your e-book. Ultimately, by actively engaging with your audience throughout the writing and publishing process, you can create a more meaningful and impactful experience for your readers while increasing the overall success of your e-book.

Chapter 9
Investing in Cryptocurrencies and Stocks:

Cryptocurrencies are digital or virtual currencies that use cryptography for security and operate independently of a central bank. They are decentralized and typically use blockchain technology to gain transparency, security, and immutability. Bitcoin, created in 2009, was the first decentralized cryptocurrency and remains the most widely used and valuable. Other popular cryptocurrencies include Ethereum, Ripple, and Litecoin. Cryptocurrencies have gained popularity as an alternative investment and a means of conducting transactions. They are also seen as a way to potentially revolutionize the financial system by providing greater financial inclusion and reducing the need for intermediaries.

Stocks, on the other hand, represent ownership in a company and are bought and sold on stock exchanges. When you buy a stock, you are buying a small piece of ownership in a company. Stocks are often considered a long-term investment and can provide investors with the opportunity to participate in a company's success through capital appreciation and dividends. They are also traded for short-term gains through speculation and market timing. Stocks are typically categorized into different sectors such as technology, healthcare, energy, and consumer goods, allowing investors to diversify their portfolios and spread their risk.

One major difference between cryptocurrencies and stocks is their underlying asset. Cryptocurrencies are digital assets that exist solely in the digital realm, while stocks represent ownership in tangible companies with physical assets and operations. Additionally, the volatility of cryptocurrencies is often much higher than that of stocks, making them a more speculative investment. While both cryptocurrencies and stocks can offer significant returns, they also come with their own set of risks and challenges.

Another key difference between cryptocurrencies and stocks is the regulatory environment in which they operate. Stocks are heavily regulated by government agencies such as the Securities and Exchange Commission (SEC) in the United States, which sets rules and standards for companies to follow. Cryptocurrencies, on the other hand, operate in a more decentralized and less regulated environment, which can lead to greater uncertainty and potential for fraud. However, this also allows for greater innovation and flexibility in the development of new financial technologies.

Investors looking to invest in cryptocurrencies should be aware of the unique risks associated with this asset class, including price volatility, security concerns, and regulatory uncertainty. On the other hand, investing in stocks requires an understanding of company fundamentals, market trends, and economic conditions. Both cryptocurrencies and stocks require careful consideration and due diligence before making any investment decisions.

Cryptocurrencies and stocks represent two distinct asset classes with their own set of characteristics, risks, and potential rewards. While cryptocurrencies offer the potential for greater innovation and financial inclusion, they also come with higher volatility and regulatory uncertainty. Stocks, on the other hand, provide ownership in tangible companies with established operations but are subject to market fluctuations and economic conditions. Both asset classes can offer opportunities for investors to grow their wealth over time, but it is important to carefully consider the unique features of each before making any investment decisions.

Investing in cryptocurrencies and stocks can be a way to grow your wealth over time, but it's important to approach it with careful consideration and understanding. Before investing in cryptocurrencies or stocks, it's important to consult with a financial advisor or investment professional to assess your individual financial situation, risk tolerance, and investment objectives. Additionally, conducting thorough research and staying informed about market trends can help you make informed investment decisions.

There are some general steps to consider when looking at making money through investing in cryptocurrencies and stocks. Educate yourself in investing in cryptocurrencies and stocks to make money, it is important to start by understanding the basics of both markets. Cryptocurrencies are digital or virtual currencies that use cryptography for security and operate independently of a central bank. Stocks, on the other hand, represent ownership in a company and are bought and sold on stock exchanges. Understanding the differences and similarities between these two types of investments is crucial for making informed decisions.

Once you have a basic understanding of cryptocurrencies and stocks, it is important to research and study the market trends. This includes analyzing historical price data, reading news articles, and following industry experts on social media platforms. By staying informed about market trends, you can make more educated decisions about when to buy or sell your investments.

In addition to market research, it is important to educate yourself on the different investment strategies that can be used in both cryptocurrency and stock markets. Some common strategies include day trading, swing trading, and long-term investing. Each strategy has its own set of risks and potential rewards, so it is important to understand the pros and cons of each before deciding which one is right for you.

Another important aspect of educating yourself in investing is the act of understanding the technology behind cryptocurrencies. Unlike stocks, which represent ownership in a company, cryptocurrencies are based on blockchain technology. Understanding how blockchain works and the unique features of different cryptocurrencies can help you make more informed investment decisions.

In addition to understanding the technology behind cryptocurrencies, it is important to be aware of the regulatory environment surrounding both cryptocurrency and stock markets. Government regulations can have a significant impact on the value of your investments, so it is important to stay informed about any changes in regulations that may affect your investments.

It is also important to educate yourself on the risks associated with investing in cryptocurrencies and stocks. Both markets are known for their volatility, which means that the value of your investments can fluctuate dramatically in a short period of time. By understanding the risks associated with each market, you can make more informed decisions about how much money to invest and when to buy or sell your investments.

In addition to understanding the risks associated with investing, it is important to have a clear understanding of your own financial goals and risk tolerance. This will help you make more informed decisions about which investments are right for you and how much money to allocate to each investment.

One of the best ways to educate yourself in investing in cryptocurrencies and stocks is to learn from others who have experience in the market. This can include reading books and articles written by industry experts, attending investment seminars and workshops, and networking with other investors. By learning from others who have experience in the market, you can gain valuable insights that can help you make more informed investment decisions.

Also setting financial goals in investing in cryptocurrencies and stocks is crucial for anyone looking to make money in the financial markets. Without clear and specific goals, it's easy to get lost in the noise and make impulsive decisions that can lead to losses. To begin with, it's important to assess your current financial situation and determine how much you can comfortably invest in cryptocurrencies and stocks. This will help you set realistic and achievable financial goals that align with your risk tolerance and investment horizon.

Once you have a clear understanding of your financial situation, it's time to set specific and measurable financial goals for your investments in cryptocurrencies and stocks. This could include setting a target return on investment, such as aiming for a certain percentage increase in your investment portfolio over a specified period of time. Additionally, you may want to set goals related to diversification, such as aiming to allocate a certain percentage of your portfolio to cryptocurrencies and stocks in different sectors or industries.

In addition to setting specific financial goals, it's important to establish a timeline for achieving these goals. This could involve setting short-term, medium-term, and long-term financial goals for your investments in cryptocurrencies and stocks. For example, you may set a short-term goal to achieve a certain percentage return on investment within the next six months, a medium-term goal to reach a specific portfolio value within the next two years, and a long-term goal to build a substantial investment portfolio for retirement.

Another important aspect of setting financial goals in investing in cryptocurrencies and stocks is to regularly review and adjust your goals as needed. The financial markets are dynamic and constantly changing, so it's essential to periodically reassess your financial goals in light of new market developments, changes in your financial situation, and shifts in your risk tolerance. By regularly reviewing and adjusting your financial goals, you can ensure that they remain relevant and achievable in the ever-evolving investment landscape.

Furthermore, it's essential to consider the level of risk you are willing to take when setting financial goals for investing in cryptocurrencies and stocks. Your risk tolerance will influence the types of investments you choose, the allocation of your investment portfolio, and the potential returns you aim to achieve. By aligning your financial goals with your risk tolerance, you can create a well-balanced investment strategy that maximizes returns while minimizing potential downside risk.

Moreover, it's beneficial to set performance benchmarks for your investments in cryptocurrencies and stocks as part of your financial goals. These benchmarks can serve as indicators of progress towards your financial goals and help you track the performance of your investment portfolio over time. By setting performance benchmarks, you can evaluate the success of your investment strategy and make informed decisions about whether adjustments are needed to stay on track towards achieving your financial goals.

In addition to setting performance benchmarks, it's important to consider the tax implications of your financial goals in investing in cryptocurrencies and stocks. Tax considerations can have a significant impact on the after-tax returns of your investments, so it's essential to factor in tax-efficient strategies when setting financial goals. This could involve aiming for specific after-tax returns on investment or implementing tax-efficient investment vehicles to optimize the tax efficiency of your investment portfolio.

Note, it's crucial to stay disciplined and focused on your financial goals when investing in cryptocurrencies and stocks. The financial markets can be volatile and unpredictable, which can lead to emotional decision-making and impulsive actions. By staying committed to your financial goals and maintaining a long-term perspective, you can avoid making rash decisions based on short-term market fluctuations and stay on course towards achieving your desired financial outcomes.

Research Investment Options: When researching investment options in cryptocurrencies and stocks to make money, it is important to start by understanding the basics of both markets. Cryptocurrencies are digital or virtual currencies that use cryptography for security and operate independently of a central bank. They are highly volatile and can offer significant returns, but also come with high risk. Stocks, on the other hand, represent ownership in a company and can provide dividends as well as capital appreciation. Understanding the differences between these two asset classes is crucial in making informed investment decisions.

Once the basics are understood, it is important to research the specific cryptocurrencies and stocks that you are interested in. For cryptocurrencies, this may involve understanding the technology behind the coin, the team behind the project, and the potential use cases for the currency. For stocks, it is important to research the company's financials, competitive positioning, and growth prospects. This research can involve reading company reports, analyst opinions, and news articles to gather as much information as possible.

In addition to researching individual assets, it is important to understand the broader market dynamics that can impact both cryptocurrencies and stocks. For cryptocurrencies, this may involve understanding trends in adoption, regulatory developments, and technological advancements. For stocks, it is important to consider macroeconomic factors, industry trends, and geopolitical events that can impact the market as a whole. By staying informed about these broader market dynamics, investors can make more informed decisions about their investments.

Another important aspect of researching investment options in cryptocurrencies and stocks is the ability to understand the risk management. Both asset classes come with inherent risks, and it is important to have a clear understanding of the risks involved in each investment. This may involve understanding the potential for loss, as well as the potential for gains, and developing a strategy for managing risk within a portfolio. This can involve diversifying across different assets, setting stop-loss orders, and having a clear exit strategy for each investment.

When researching investment options in cryptocurrencies and stocks, it is also important to consider the role of technology in investing. In recent years, technological advancements have made it easier than ever for individual investors to access and analyze investment opportunities. This can involve using online platforms to research and trade assets, as well as using tools such as algorithmic trading and robo-advisors to help make investment decisions. Understanding how to leverage technology in investing can help investors make more informed decisions and stay ahead of market trends.

In addition to technology, it is also important to consider the role of regulation when researching investment options in cryptocurrencies and stocks. Both markets are subject to regulatory oversight, and understanding the regulatory environment is crucial in making informed investment decisions. This may involve understanding the legal status of cryptocurrencies in different jurisdictions, as well as staying informed about changes in securities regulations that can impact stock investments. By staying informed about regulatory developments, investors can better navigate the legal landscape and make more informed investment decisions.

Furthermore, it is important to consider the long-term outlook when researching investment options in cryptocurrencies and stocks. While short-term price movements can be influenced by market sentiment and speculation, it is important to consider the long-term fundamentals of each investment. This may involve considering factors such as the potential for long-term growth, the sustainability of a company's competitive advantages, and the potential for widespread adoption of a cryptocurrency. By focusing on the long-term outlook, investors can make more informed decisions that align with their overall investment goals.

When researching investment options in cryptocurrencies and stocks, it is important to seek out diverse sources of information. This can involve reading a variety of news sources, following industry experts on social media, and participating in online forums and communities dedicated to investing. By seeking out diverse perspectives and staying open to new ideas, investors can gain a more comprehensive understanding of the opportunities and risks involved in both cryptocurrency and stock investments.

Other ways include diversifying your portfolio in investing in cryptocurrencies and stocks is a smart strategy to manage risk and potentially increase returns. By spreading your investments across different asset classes, you can reduce the impact of any one investment underperforming. When it comes to cryptocurrencies, it's important to consider factors such as market volatility, regulatory changes, and technological advancements. In contrast, stocks offer the potential for long-term growth and income through dividends. By combining these two asset classes, you can create a well-rounded portfolio that balances risk and reward.

One way to diversify your portfolio in cryptocurrencies is to invest in a mix of large-cap and small-cap coins. Large-cap coins such as Bitcoin and Ethereum are more established and have a higher market capitalization, while small-cap coins have the potential for higher growth but also come with greater risk. Additionally, consider diversifying across different sectors within the cryptocurrency market, such as decentralized finance (DeFi), non-fungible tokens (NFTs), and blockchain infrastructure projects. This can help spread risk and capture opportunities in different areas of the market.

In terms of stocks, diversification can be achieved by investing in a mix of industries and sectors. For example, you might consider allocating funds to technology companies, healthcare providers, consumer goods manufacturers, and financial institutions. By spreading your investments across different sectors, you can reduce the impact of sector-specific risks and potentially benefit from the growth of multiple industries. Additionally, consider investing in both domestic and international stocks to further diversify your portfolio geographically.

Another way to diversify your portfolio in cryptocurrencies and stocks is by considering the correlation between different assets. For example, Bitcoin and gold have historically had a low correlation, meaning they tend to move independently of each other. By including assets with low correlation in your portfolio, you can further reduce risk and potentially enhance returns. Similarly, when investing in stocks, consider the correlation between different industries and sectors to ensure that your portfolio is well diversified.

In addition to considering the correlation between assets, it's important to rebalance your portfolio regularly to maintain diversification. As the value of different assets fluctuates, your portfolio's allocation may shift over time. Rebalancing involves selling assets that have performed well and buying assets that have underperformed in order to maintain your desired asset allocation. By regularly rebalancing your portfolio, you can ensure that your investments remain diversified and aligned with your risk tolerance and investment goals.

Furthermore, consider incorporating alternative investments into your portfolio to further diversify your holdings. Alternative investments such as real estate, commodities, and private equity can offer returns that are not closely correlated with traditional asset classes like stocks and bonds. By including alternative investments in your portfolio, you can reduce overall risk and potentially enhance returns through exposure to different market dynamics.

When diversifying your portfolio in cryptocurrencies and stocks, it's important to consider your investment time horizon and risk tolerance. For long-term investors with a higher risk tolerance, a more aggressive allocation to cryptocurrencies may be appropriate, while conservative investors may prefer a more balanced approach with a larger allocation to stocks. Ultimately, the key to successful diversification is to construct a portfolio that aligns with your individual financial goals and investment strategy while managing risk effectively.

Please note that diversifying your portfolio in cryptocurrencies and stocks can help manage risk and potentially enhance returns by spreading investments across different asset classes, industries, and geographic regions. By investing in a mix of large-cap and small-cap cryptocurrencies, diversifying across sectors, considering correlation between assets, regularly rebalancing your portfolio, incorporating alternative investments, and aligning your allocation with your investment time horizon and risk tolerance, you can create a well-rounded portfolio that balances risk and reward. It's important to conduct thorough research and seek professional advice when constructing a diversified portfolio to ensure it aligns with your financial goals and investment strategy.

In addition to the above said, it is also very vital to note that when choosing an investment strategy for cryptocurrencies and stocks, it's important to consider your financial goals, risk tolerance, and investment timeline. One key factor to consider is diversification. Diversifying your investments across different cryptocurrencies and stocks can help spread out risk and potentially increase returns. Additionally, consider the volatility of the market and how much risk you are willing to take on. If you have a higher risk tolerance, you may be more inclined to invest in more volatile assets such as cryptocurrencies. However, if you have a lower risk tolerance, you may prefer to focus on more stable stocks.

Another important aspect to consider when choosing an investment strategy is conducting thorough research. This includes understanding the fundamentals of the cryptocurrencies and stocks you are interested in, as well as staying informed about market trends and news. By staying informed, you can make more informed investment decisions and potentially identify opportunities for growth.

Furthermore, it's crucial to have a clear understanding of your investment timeline. Are you looking for short-term gains or long-term growth? Your investment strategy should align with your timeline. For example, if you are investing in cryptocurrencies for long-term growth, you may take a buy-and-hold approach, whereas if you are trading stocks for short-term gains, you may take a more active trading approach.

Additionally, consider the role of technology and innovation in the cryptocurrency and stock markets. As these markets continue to evolve, it's important to stay abreast of technological advancements and how they may impact your investment strategy. For example, advancements in blockchain technology may present new opportunities for investing in cryptocurrencies, while technological innovations in various industries may impact stock performance.

Moreover, it's important to consider the role of macroeconomic factors in your investment strategy. Factors such as interest rates, inflation, and geopolitical events can impact the performance of both cryptocurrencies and stocks. By staying informed about these macroeconomic factors, you can make more informed investment decisions and potentially mitigate risk.

Another consideration when choosing an investment strategy is the use of technical analysis and fundamental analysis. Technical analysis involves analyzing price charts and patterns to identify potential entry and exit points, while fundamental analysis involves evaluating the financial health and performance of companies or cryptocurrencies. By using a combination of these analyses, you can make more informed investment decisions.

Furthermore, it's important to consider the impact of regulations on cryptocurrencies and stocks. As regulatory environments continue to evolve, it's important to stay informed about any regulatory changes that may impact your investments. By staying informed about regulations, you can make more informed investment decisions and potentially mitigate regulatory risk.

Consider seeking professional advice when choosing an investment strategy. Consulting with a financial advisor or investment professional can provide valuable insights and guidance as you navigate the complex world of investing in cryptocurrencies and stocks. A professional can help you assess your financial goals, risk tolerance, and investment timeline, and develop a tailored investment strategy that aligns with your needs. Remember that all investments carry inherent risks, and it's important to conduct thorough research and seek professional advice before making investment decisions. Additionally, regulations and market conditions for crypto-currencies and stocks can vary widely by region, so it's important to be aware of local laws and regulations governing investment activities.

Remember the importance of having an investment account channelled to your business. Opening an investment account for investing in cryptocurrencies and stocks can be a great way to build wealth and secure your financial future. To begin, you'll need to choose a reputable and reliable brokerage or exchange platform that offers the ability to invest in both cryptocurrencies and stocks. Look for platforms that offer a wide range of investment options, competitive fees, and strong security measures to protect your assets.

Once you've chosen a platform, you'll need to create an account by providing personal information such as your name, address, and social security number. You may also need to provide additional documentation to verify your identity, such as a driver's license or passport. It's important to ensure that the platform you choose complies with all relevant regulations and has strong security measures in place to protect your personal information and assets.

After creating your account, you'll need to fund it in order to start investing. Most platforms offer a variety of funding options, such as bank transfers, credit/debit card payments, and wire transfers. Choose the option that works best for you and follow the instructions provided by the platform to complete the funding process. Keep in mind that some funding methods may incur fees or have processing times, so be sure to factor these into your investment strategy.

Once your account is funded, you can start investing in cryptocurrencies and stocks. Do your research and consider working with a financial advisor to develop a diversified investment portfolio that aligns with your financial goals and risk tolerance. When investing in cryptocurrencies, be sure to carefully consider the unique risks and volatility associated with this asset class, and consider starting with a small allocation until you become more familiar with the market.

As you begin investing, it's important to stay informed about market trends and developments that may impact your investments. Keep an eye on news and market analysis, and consider setting up alerts or notifications to stay updated on the performance of your investments. Regularly review your investment portfolio and consider making adjustments as needed to ensure that it remains aligned with your financial goals and risk tolerance.

In addition to investing in individual cryptocurrencies and stocks, you may also consider investing in exchange-traded funds (ETFs) or mutual funds that offer exposure to these asset classes. These investment vehicles can provide diversification and professional management, making them a convenient option for investors who prefer a hands-off approach to investing.

In this regards, it is important to monitor the performance of your investments and stay disciplined in your investment strategy. Avoid making impulsive decisions based on short-term market fluctuations, and instead focus on the long-term growth potential of your investments. Consider setting specific investment goals and regularly review your progress towards achieving them. By staying informed, diversifying your investments, and maintaining a disciplined approach, you can build a strong investment portfolio that aligns with your financial goals.

Monitoring the market trend in investing in cryptocurrencies and stocks is crucial for making informed decisions and maximizing returns. There are several strategies and tools that investors can utilize to stay updated on the market trends. One effective way to monitor the market trend is by staying informed through financial news outlets, such as Bloomberg, CNBC, and Reuters. These platforms provide up-to-date information on market movements, economic indicators, and company news that can impact the price of cryptocurrencies and stocks. By following these news outlets, investors can gain valuable insights into market trends and make informed decisions about their investment portfolios.

Another important strategy for monitoring market trends is to utilize technical analysis tools to track price movements and identify potential entry and exit points. Technical analysis tools, such as moving averages, relative strength index (RSI), and Bollinger Bands, can help investors identify trends, support and resistance levels, and overbought or oversold conditions. By using these tools, investors can make more informed decisions about when to buy or sell cryptocurrencies and stocks based on market trends and price movements.

In addition to technical analysis tools, investors can also utilize fundamental analysis to monitor market trends. Fundamental analysis involves evaluating the financial health and performance of companies, as well as macroeconomic factors that can impact the market. By analyzing factors such as earnings reports, revenue growth, and industry trends, investors can gain a better understanding of the underlying value of stocks and cryptocurrencies, and identify potential market trends that could impact their investment decisions.

Furthermore, investors can also monitor market trends by keeping an eye on social media and online forums where discussions about cryptocurrencies and stocks take place. Platforms such as Twitter, Reddit, and stock trading forums can provide valuable insights into market sentiment, investor behaviour, and emerging trends that may impact the market. By staying engaged with these online communities, investors can gain a better understanding of market trends and make more informed decisions about their investment strategies.

Moreover, it is important for investors to keep an eye on regulatory developments and government policies that can impact the cryptocurrency and stock markets. Regulatory changes, such as new legislation or government interventions, can have a significant impact on market trends and investor sentiment. By staying informed about regulatory developments, investors can anticipate potential market trends and adjust their investment strategies accordingly.

Another effective way to monitor market trends is by analyzing historical data and market patterns to identify recurring trends and potential market cycles. By studying historical price movements and market patterns, investors can gain valuable insights into potential market trends and make more informed decisions about their investment strategies. Additionally, investors can also utilize market indicators, such as the VIX (volatility index) or the put/call ratio, to gauge market sentiment and potential trends.

Furthermore, it is important for investors to stay updated on global economic developments and geopolitical events that can impact the cryptocurrency and stock markets. Economic indicators, such as GDP growth, inflation rates, and unemployment data, can provide valuable insights into the health of the economy and potential market trends. Additionally, geopolitical events, such as trade tensions or geopolitical conflicts, can also impact market trends and investor sentiment. By staying informed about global economic developments and geopolitical events, investors can anticipate potential market trends and make more informed decisions about their investment portfolios.

It is important to know that monitoring the market trend in investing in cryptocurrencies and stocks is essential for making informed investment decisions. By staying informed through financial news outlets, utilizing technical and fundamental analysis tools, staying engaged with online communities, monitoring regulatory developments, analyzing historical data and market patterns, and staying updated on global economic and geopolitical events, investors can gain valuable insights into potential market trends and make more informed decisions about their investment strategies.

Managing risk is crucial for long-term success when investing in any business. One of the most important ways to manage risk is through diversification. By spreading your investments across different cryptocurrencies and stocks, you can reduce the impact of a single investment performing poorly. Diversification can help protect your portfolio from significant losses and provide more stability over time.

Another key aspect of managing risk in cryptocurrency and stock investing is conducting thorough research. Before investing in any asset, it's essential to understand the market, the technology behind the cryptocurrency, or the fundamentals of the company's stock. By staying informed and conducting due diligence, you can make more informed investment decisions and reduce the risk of potential losses.

These are important because setting clear investment goals and sticking to a well-defined strategy is also crucial for managing risk. Whether you're investing in cryptocurrencies or stocks, having a clear understanding of your risk tolerance, investment timeframe, and target returns can help you make more rational decisions and avoid emotional investing. Establishing a solid investment plan can help you stay focused on your long-term objectives and will also reduce the impact of short-term market fluctuations.

Setting clear investment goals, it's important to regularly review and adjust your investment portfolio. Market conditions can change rapidly and what may have been a sound investment strategy in the past may no longer be suitable for the current market environment. By periodically reviewing your portfolio and making adjustments as needed, you can adapt to changing market conditions and reduce the risk of significant losses.

Implementing risk management tools, such as stop-loss orders and limit orders, can also help mitigate potential losses when investing in cryptocurrencies and stocks. These tools allow investors to set predetermined price levels at which they are willing to buy or sell an asset, helping to limit losses and protect profits. By using risk management tools effectively, investors can minimize the impact of market volatility and reduce the potential for significant losses.

Staying disciplined and avoiding impulsive decisions is another important aspect of managing risk in cryptocurrency and stock investing. Emotional reactions to market fluctuations can lead to irrational decision-making and increase the risk of significant losses. By staying disciplined and sticking to your investment strategy, you can avoid making hasty decisions based on short-term market movements and reduce the impact of emotional investing on your portfolio.

To a greater extent, considering the impact of external factors, such as regulatory developments and geopolitical events, is essential for managing risk in cryptocurrency and stock investing. These external factors can have a significant impact on market sentiment and asset prices, leading to increased volatility and potential losses. By staying informed about external developments and considering their potential impact on your investments, you can make more informed decisions and reduce the risk of significant losses.

Special way to achieve more is by reinvesting profits when investing in cryptocurrencies and stocks. This is crucial strategy for long-term wealth building. By reinvesting profits, investors can maximize their returns and compound their gains over time. There are several effective ways to reinvest profits, including dividend reinvestment plans, automatic investment plans, and simply using the profits to purchase more shares or cryptocurrencies. Regardless of the method chosen, the key is to consistently reinvest profits to take advantage of the power of compounding.

One effective strategy for reinvesting profits in stocks is to enrol in a dividend reinvestment plan (DRIP). With a DRIP, any dividends earned from the stocks are automatically reinvested to purchase additional shares. This allows investors to gradually increase their holdings without incurring additional transaction costs. Over time, the compounded effect of reinvested dividends can significantly boost the overall return on investment.

Another approach for reinvesting profits in stocks is to set up an automatic investment plan. With this strategy, a predetermined amount of profits is automatically reinvested at regular intervals, such as monthly or quarterly. This approach helps investors avoid the temptation to spend profits and ensures that the money is put back to work in the market. Additionally, automatic investment plans can help smooth out market volatility by dollar-cost averaging into the market over time.

In the realm of cryptocurrencies, reinvesting profits can be achieved by using the gains to purchase additional coins or tokens. As with stocks, reinvesting profits in cryptocurrencies can be a powerful way to compound gains over time. Investors can choose to allocate a certain percentage of their profits to reinvestment, or they can reinvest the entire amount to maximize the potential for growth.

One important consideration when reinvesting profits in both stocks and cryptocurrencies is to carefully evaluate the potential for future growth. While it can be tempting to immediately reinvest all profits, it's essential to conduct thorough research and analysis to identify the most promising investment opportunities. By focusing on high-quality assets with strong growth potential, investors can maximize the impact of their reinvested profits.

Additionally, diversification is a key principle to keep in mind when reinvesting profits. Instead of putting all profits back into a single stock or cryptocurrency, it's wise to spread the reinvested funds across a diversified portfolio. This approach can help mitigate risk and enhance overall portfolio stability, especially in volatile market conditions.

Furthermore, investors should consider their long-term financial goals when deciding how to reinvest profits. Whether the objective is to build wealth for retirement, fund future expenses, or achieve other financial milestones, aligning the reinvestment strategy with these goals is essential. By maintaining a clear focus on long-term objectives, investors can make more informed decisions about how to effectively reinvest their profits.

In conclusion, reinvesting profits when investing in cryptocurrencies and stocks is a powerful wealth-building strategy that can significantly enhance overall returns in the business; whether through dividend reinvestment plans, automatic investment plans, or simply purchasing more shares or cryptocurrencies, the key is to consistently reinvest profits and take advantage of the power of compounding. By carefully evaluating investment opportunities, diversifying across assets, and aligning with long-term financial goals, investors can make the most of their reinvested profits and set themselves up for long-term success in the market.

I reality, extar care must be taken when investing money in any form of business.

Disadvantages of investing in Cryptocurrency:

Investing in cryptocurrency business comes with several disadvantages. One major drawback is the high volatility of the cryptocurrency market. Prices of cryptocurrencies can fluctuate dramatically within a short period of time, leading to potential losses for investors. This volatility makes it difficult to predict the future value of a particular cryptocurrency, making it a risky investment option.

Another disadvantage of investing in cryptocurrency business is the lack of regulation and security. Unlike traditional financial markets, the cryptocurrency market is largely unregulated, which exposes investors to potential fraud and security breaches. There have been numerous cases of hacking and theft in the cryptocurrency space, leading to significant financial losses for investors.

Additionally, investing in cryptocurrency business requires a certain level of technical knowledge and understanding of blockchain technology. For many investors, especially those unfamiliar with the technical aspects of cryptocurrencies, navigating the complex world of digital assets can be challenging and daunting. This lack of understanding can lead to poor investment decisions and ultimately result in financial losses.

Chapter 10
Participating in Online Marketplaces for Services:

Participating in online marketplaces for services involves engaging in the buying and selling of services through digital platforms. These platforms connect service providers with customers, enabling convenient and efficient transactions. Service providers can showcase their skills and expertise, while customers can easily browse and compare different offerings. Online marketplaces for services encompass a wide range of industries, including freelance work, consulting, tutoring, graphic design, programming, and more.

The participation in online marketplaces for services has several advantages. For service providers, it offers the opportunity to reach a broader customer base and expand their business globally. It also provides flexibility and autonomy, allowing them to work on their own terms and set their own rates. For customers, online marketplaces offer convenience, accessibility, and the ability to compare multiple service providers before making a decision.

To participate in online marketplaces for services, individuals typically create a profile on the platform, showcasing their skills, experience, and portfolio. They may also set their availability, rates, and terms of service. Customers can then browse through the profiles, read reviews, and contact service providers to discuss their needs and negotiate terms.

Participating in online marketplaces for services can be a rewarding experience for both service providers and customers. However, it's important to carefully research and select reputable platforms, as well as to follow the platform's guidelines and terms of service to ensure a smooth and successful experience.

Here are the steps to consider when looking at making money by participating in online marketplaces for services:

Identify Your Skills: Determine the skills and expertise you have that can be offered as a service. This could include writing, graphic design, web development, digital marketing, virtual assistance, and more.

Research Online Marketplaces: Explore online marketplaces such as Upwork, Fiverr, Freelancer, Guru, and TaskRabbit where you can offer your services. Compare the features, fees, and user base of different platforms to find the best fit for your skills.

Create a Profile: Set up a professional profile on the chosen online marketplace. Highlight your skills, experience, portfolio, and any relevant certifications or qualifications.

Define Your Services: Clearly define the services you are offering, including the scope of work, deliverables, and pricing. Consider offering packages or tiered pricing to cater to different client needs.

Showcase Your Work: Upload samples of your previous work or projects to showcase your skills and expertise. This can help potential clients understand the quality of your services.

Set Competitive Prices: Research the pricing of similar services on the platform and set competitive prices for your offerings. Consider starting with competitive rates to attract initial clients and build a positive reputation.

Provide Excellent Customer Service: Communicate promptly and professionally with potential clients and deliver high-quality work within agreed-upon timelines. Positive client reviews and ratings can help attract more clients in the future.

Promote Your Services: Use social media and professional networks to promote your services and share client testimonials or success stories. Networking and word-of-mouth referrals can also help attract new clients.

Expand Your Offerings: Consider expanding your service offerings based on client demand and industry trends. This can help you attract a wider range of clients and increase your earning potential.

Manage Your Reputation: Maintain a positive reputation by delivering high-quality work, addressing client feedback, and resolving any issues professionally.

Analyze Performance: Use analytics tools provided by the platform to track your performance, client satisfaction, and earnings. Use this data to optimize your service offerings and pricing strategy.

By following these steps and consistently delivering high-quality services, you can build a successful freelance business through online marketplaces.

Chapter 11
Selling Handmade Products on E-commerce Platforms:

E-commerce, short for electronic commerce, refers to the buying and selling of goods and services over the internet. It has revolutionized the way businesses operate and how consumers shop. E-commerce encompasses a wide range of activities, including online retail, electronic payments, online auctions, and internet banking. It has become an integral part of the global economy, allowing businesses to reach customers around the world and enabling consumers to access a vast array of products and services from the comfort of their own homes.

One of the key features of e-commerce is its ability to provide a convenient and efficient shopping experience for consumers. With just a few clicks, shoppers can browse through a vast selection of products, compare prices, and make purchases without ever leaving their homes. This convenience has led to the rapid growth of online retail, with e-commerce sales accounting for an increasing share of total retail sales each year. In addition to convenience, e-commerce also offers consumers' access to a wider variety of products and services than traditional brick-and-mortar stores, as online retailers can stock and sell an almost unlimited range of items without the physical constraints of a traditional store.

E-commerce has also transformed the way businesses operate, allowing them to reach customers in new and innovative ways. With an online presence, businesses can expand their reach beyond their local market and tap into a global customer base. This has opened up new opportunities for small businesses and entrepreneurs, who can now compete on a more level playing field with larger, established companies. E-commerce has also enabled businesses to streamline their operations and reduce costs by automating processes such as inventory management, order processing, and customer service.

In addition to its impact on retail, e-commerce has also revolutionized the way people conduct financial transactions. Online banking and electronic payment systems have made it easier than ever for consumers to manage their finances and make purchases. This has led to a decrease in the use of cash and checks, as more and more people turn to electronic forms of payment. E-commerce has also facilitated the growth of online marketplaces and auction sites, where individuals can buy and sell goods and services directly with one another, further expanding the reach and impact of e-commerce on the global economy.

E-commerce has also had a profound impact on the way businesses market and advertise their products and services. With the rise of social media and digital advertising, businesses can now reach potential customers through targeted online campaigns, reaching specific demographics with personalized messages. This has allowed businesses to create more engaging and interactive marketing strategies, leading to increased brand awareness and customer engagement. E-commerce has also enabled businesses to gather valuable data on consumer behaviour and preferences, allowing them to tailor their marketing efforts to better meet the needs and desires of their target audience.

The growth of e-commerce has also led to the development of new business models and strategies. Subscription-based services, for example, have become increasingly popular in the e-commerce space, offering consumers access to a wide range of products or services for a recurring fee. This model has proven successful for businesses in various industries, from streaming services to meal delivery companies, as it provides a predictable revenue stream and fosters customer loyalty. Additionally, e-commerce has given rise to new forms of entrepreneurship, such as dropshipping and affiliate marketing, which allow individuals to start their own online businesses with minimal upfront investment.

E-commerce has also had a significant impact on logistics and supply chain management. With the rise of e-commerce, there has been an increased demand for fast and reliable shipping services to deliver products to customers around the world. This has led to innovations in logistics technology and infrastructure, such as automated warehouses and advanced tracking systems, to meet the growing demands of e-commerce. Additionally, e-commerce has driven changes in inventory management practices, as businesses seek to optimize their supply chains to meet the demands of online retail and ensure efficient order fulfilment.

E-commerce has fundamentally transformed the way businesses operate and how consumers shop. It has provided unparalleled convenience and access to a wide range of products and services for consumers, while enabling businesses to reach new customers and streamline their operations. The impact of e-commerce extends beyond retail, influencing financial transactions, marketing strategies, business models, entrepreneurship, and supply chain management. As e-commerce continues to evolve and grow, it will undoubtedly shape the future of commerce and have a lasting impact on the global economy.

Selling handmade products on e-commerce platforms can be a rewarding way to make money, by showcasing your creativity and craftsmanship. Certainly! Selling handmade products on e-commerce platforms has become increasingly popular in recent years, offering a great opportunity for artisans and crafters to reach a wider audience and generate income. Here's a comprehensive overview of this concept:

Selling handmade products on e-commerce platforms involves creating and selling unique, handcrafted items through online marketplaces. These platforms provide a virtual storefront for artisans to showcase their products, manage inventory, process payments, and ship orders to customers worldwide.

The benefits of using E-commerce platforms are as follows:

- Wider Reach: E-commerce platforms offer a global reach, allowing artisans to sell their products to customers beyond their local markets.
- Convenience: Customers can conveniently browse and purchase handmade products from the comfort of their homes.
- Reduced Costs: Selling online eliminates the need for physical storefronts, reducing overhead costs for artisans.
- Increased Visibility: E-commerce platforms provide artisans with tools to promote their products and build a customer base through online marketing and social media integration.

Here are the steps to consider when looking at making money by selling handmade products on e-commerce platforms:

Identify Your Niche: Determine the type of handmade products you want to sell. This could include jewelry, clothing, accessories, home decor, art, crafts, or any other handmade items that showcase your skills and creativity.

Research E-commerce Platforms: Explore e-commerce platforms such as Etsy, Amazon Handmade, eBay, and Shopify that cater to sellers of handmade products. Compare the features, fees, and audience of different platforms to find the best fit for your products.

Create a Brand: Develop a unique brand identity for your handmade products. This includes creating a brand name, logo, and visual style that reflects the essence of your products.

Develop Your Products: Create high-quality handmade products that are unique and reflect your craftsmanship. Ensure that your products are well-crafted, visually appealing, and offer value to potential customers.

Set Up an Online Store: Create an online store on the chosen e-commerce platform to showcase and sell your handmade products. Customize your store to reflect your brand and product offerings.

Product Photography: Take high-quality photographs of your handmade products that showcase them in the best light. Clear, well-lit images are essential for attracting potential buyers.

Write Compelling Product Descriptions: Craft detailed and compelling product descriptions that highlight the unique features, materials used, and the story behind each handmade product.

Set Competitive Prices: Research the pricing of similar handmade products on the platform and set competitive prices for your offerings. Consider the time, effort, and materials invested in creating each product when setting prices.

Promote Your Products: Use social media, content marketing, and email marketing to promote your handmade products. Showcase your creative process, share behind-the-scenes glimpses, and engage with potential customers.

Provide Excellent Customer Service: Offer responsive customer service, address inquiries promptly, and ensure timely order fulfilment. Positive customer experiences can lead to repeat business and word-of-mouth referrals.

Expand Your Product Line: Consider expanding your product offerings based on customer feedback and market demand. This can help you attract a wider range of customers and increase your earning potential.

Analyze Performance: Use analytics tools provided by the e-commerce platform to track the performance of your store, customer engagement, and sales data. Use this data to optimize your product offerings and marketing strategy.

By following these steps and consistently delivering high-quality handmade products, you can build a successful business selling handmade items on e-commerce platforms.

Chapter 12
Monetizing Photography and Artwork Online:

Photographs are visual representations captured through the use of a camera, capturing a moment in time. They can be used to tell a story, evoke emotions, or simply document a specific moment or scene. Photographs can be created using various techniques such as long exposure, macro photography, or portrait photography, each offering a unique perspective on the subject. Photographs can be used for personal enjoyment, commercial purposes, or artistic expression.

Artwork is a broad term that encompasses various forms of creative expression, including paintings, drawings, sculptures, and digital art. Artwork is a visual representation of an artist's imagination, emotions, and experiences. It can be used to convey a message, provoke thought, or simply serve as a form of aesthetic enjoyment. Artwork can be created using a wide range of mediums and techniques, allowing artists to explore their creativity and express themselves in unique ways.

Making money using photographs and artwork can be achieved through various avenues. One common way is by selling prints of photographs or artwork through online platforms or at art fairs and exhibitions. Artists and photographers can also license their work for use in advertising, editorial content or commercial products. Additionally, creating commissioned pieces for clients or collaborating with brands for creative projects can be lucrative opportunities to generate income.

Another way to make money using photographs and artwork is by offering services such as portrait photography, event photography, or custom artwork commissions. Many individuals and businesses are willing to pay for professional photography services for special occasions or to enhance their branding with custom artwork. Additionally, artists and photographers can teach workshops, offer online courses, or provide mentorship to aspiring creative looking to improve their skills and knowledge in the field.

Furthermore, leveraging social media platforms and online marketplaces can be an effective way to sell photographs and artwork directly to a global audience. Building a strong online presence through platforms like Instagram, Etsy, or Behance can help artists and photographers reach potential customers and showcase their work to a wider audience. Utilizing e-commerce platforms to sell prints, digital downloads, or merchandise featuring their artwork can also be a profitable venture.

In addition to selling physical prints or digital downloads of photographs and artwork, artists and photographers can explore opportunities in the stock photography and art licensing industry. By submitting their work to stock agencies or licensing platforms, they can earn royalties from the use of their images in various commercial and editorial projects. This passive income stream allows artists and photographers to earn money from their existing portfolio while focusing on creating new work.

Collaborating with galleries, art dealers, or art consultants can also provide opportunities for artists to exhibit and sell their artwork to collectors and art enthusiasts. Participating in art shows, exhibitions, and art fairs can help artists gain exposure and connect with potential buyers interested in investing in their work. Building relationships with art professionals and collectors can open doors to lucrative opportunities for selling artwork and expanding one's artistic career.

Lastly, artists and photographers can monetize their expertise and experience by offering consulting services, public speaking engagements, or writing articles/books about their creative process and industry insights. Sharing knowledge and insights through workshops, seminars, or written content can not only generate income but also establish them as thought leaders in their respective fields. By diversifying their revenue streams and leveraging their skills and expertise, artists and photographers can create sustainable income opportunities using their photographs and artwork.

Monetizing photography and artwork online can be a fulfilling way to earn income by showcasing your creative talents. This is the process of generating revenue from creative works such as photographs and artwork.

Places to Monetize Photographs include but not limited to:

1. Stock Photography: Sell your photos to stock photography websites like Shutterstock or Alamy, where customers can purchase and use them for various purposes.
2. Freelance Photography: Offer your photography services to clients for events, weddings, portraits, product photography, and more.
3. Prints and Wall Art: Sell physical prints of your photographs, framed or unframed, through your own website or online platforms like Etsy.
4. Photo Licensing: License your photos for use in advertisements, magazines, websites, and other media for a fee.

> Remember, building a successful revenue stream from photography or artwork requires dedication, consistency, and effective marketing strategies. Research your target audience, understand market trends, and continuously create high-quality work to attract buyers and collectors.

I

Here are the steps to consider when looking at making money by monetizing photographs and artworks online.

Create High-Quality Content: Develop a portfolio of high-quality photography and artwork that showcases your skills, creativity, and unique style. This can include photographs, digital art, paintings, illustrations, and other visual creations.

Choose Your Medium: Determine the medium through which you want to monetize your photography and artwork. This could include print-on-demand services, stock photography platforms, art marketplaces, or your own e-commerce store.

Research Online Platforms: Explore online platforms such as Adobe Stock, Shutterstock, Etsy, Society6, and Fine Art America that cater to photographers and artists. Compare the features, fees, and audience of different platforms to find the best fit for your work.

Set Up an Online Portfolio: Create an online portfolio to showcase your photography and artwork. This can be a website, a profile on an art marketplace, or a gallery on a print-on-demand platform.

Protect Your Work: Consider copyrighting your original artwork and photographs to protect them from unauthorized use or reproduction.

Offer Prints and Products: Utilize print-on-demand services to offer prints of your artwork and photographs on various products such as posters, canvas prints, phone cases, apparel, and more. This allows you to reach a wider audience and monetize your work through product sales.

Sell Digital Downloads: Offer digital downloads of your artwork or photographs for personal or commercial use. This can be done through platforms that specialize in digital downloads for creative content.

License Your Work: Consider licensing your photography and artwork for commercial use. This can include selling licenses for specific uses such as advertising, editorial content, or product packaging.

Promote Your Work: Use social media, content marketing, and email marketing to promote your photography and artwork. Showcase your creative process, share behind-the-scenes glimpses, and engage with potential customers.

Provide Excellent Customer Service: Offer responsive customer service, address inquiries promptly, and ensure timely order fulfilment. Positive customer experiences can lead to repeat business and word-of-mouth referrals.

Collaborate with Brands: Explore collaborations with brands and companies for sponsored content or brand partnerships. This can involve creating custom artwork or photography for specific campaigns or products.

Analyze Performance: Use analytics tools provided by the platform to track the performance of your portfolio, sales data, customer engagement, and revenue generated from your photography and artwork.

By following these steps and consistently showcasing your creativity through high-quality photography and artwork, you can work towards monetizing your creative talents online.

Chapter 13
Engaging in Virtual Real Estate and Domain Flipping:

Virtual estate refers to the online properties such as websites, domain names, and digital assets that can be bought, sold, and developed for profit. In the digital world, virtual estate is the equivalent of real estate in the physical world. Domain flipping, on the other hand, is the practice of buying domain names at a low price and then selling them at a higher price for profit. Both virtual estate and domain flipping are popular methods of making money online and have become lucrative opportunities for entrepreneurs and investors.

In the world of virtual estate, the value of a website or domain name is determined by various factors such as its traffic, revenue potential, brandability, and market demand. Just like in real estate, location is key. A domain name that is short, memorable, and relevant to a popular niche can fetch a high price in the market. Similarly, a website with high traffic, quality content, and a strong brand presence can be sold for a substantial amount. The art of virtual estate lies in identifying undervalued online properties and maximizing their potential to increase their market value.

Domain flipping, on the other hand, involves the strategic acquisition and resale of domain names. This practice requires a keen understanding of market trends, keyword popularity, and branding potential. Successful domain flippers are able to identify valuable domain names that are currently undervalued and have the potential to appreciate in the future. They then acquire these domains at a low price and sell them at a higher price to interested buyers. Domain flipping can be a profitable venture for those who are able to spot valuable domain names before they become mainstream.

One of the key strategies in virtual estate and domain flipping is to conduct thorough research and analysis before making any investment. This involves identifying niche markets with high demand, understanding keyword trends, and evaluating the potential for future growth. By staying informed about industry developments and consumer behavior, virtual estate investors and domain flippers can make informed decisions about which properties to acquire and develop for maximum profit.

In addition to buying and selling virtual estate and domain names, another method of making money online in this field is through development and monetization. This involves acquiring underdeveloped websites or domain names and improving their content, design, and functionality to increase their value. Once the properties have been enhanced, they can be monetized through various methods such as advertising, affiliate marketing, or selling products and services. This approach allows entrepreneurs to generate recurring income from their virtual estate investments while also increasing their long-term resale value.

Furthermore, virtual estate and domain flipping offer opportunities for creative entrepreneurship and innovation. In today's digital economy, there is a growing demand for unique online properties and brandable domain names. Entrepreneurs who are able to identify emerging trends and consumer needs can capitalize on this demand by creating valuable digital assets that resonate with their target audience. By leveraging their creativity and strategic vision, they can develop virtual estate that not only generates immediate revenue but also becomes a valuable long-term asset.

Moreover, virtual estate and domain flipping provide a global platform for investors and entrepreneurs to participate in the digital economy. Unlike traditional real estate, virtual estate investments are not limited by geographical boundaries. This means that individuals from all over the world can buy, sell, and develop online properties without being restricted by location. The borderless nature of virtual estate and domain flipping allows for greater accessibility and diversity in investment opportunities, making it an attractive option for those seeking to diversify their portfolio and generate income from the digital marketplace.

In conclusion, virtual estate and domain flipping are lucrative methods of making money online that offer diverse opportunities for investment, development, and innovation. By understanding the principles of virtual real estate valuation, market trends, and consumer behavior, entrepreneurs and investors can leverage their knowledge to identify valuable online properties and domain names. Whether through strategic acquisition, development, or creative entrepreneurship, virtual estate and domain flipping provide a dynamic platform for individuals to participate in the digital economy and generate sustainable income from their online investments.

Engaging in virtual real estate and domain flipping can be a lucrative way to make money by investing in digital assets. Here are the steps to consider when looking at make money through virtual real estate and domain flipping:

Research the Market: Gain an understanding of the virtual real estate and domain market. Stay informed about current trends, popular niches, and the value of different types of digital assets.

Identify Profitable Niches: Determine which niches or industries are in high demand for virtual real estate and domain names. This could include niches such as technology, finance, health, lifestyle, and more.

Domain Research: Research and identify domain names that have potential value. Look for domains that are short, memorable, brand-able, and relevant to popular keywords or industry-specific terms.

Purchase Virtual Real Estate: Invest in virtual real estate such as digital properties within virtual worlds, met-averse platforms, or other digital environments. Consider properties with high potential for development or resale.

Domain Acquisition: Acquire domain names through domain marketplaces, auctions, or direct purchases from domain owners. Look for undervalued domains with potential for rebranding or resale.

Develop a Portfolio: Build a portfolio of virtual real estate properties and domain names that have potential for appreciation in value. Diversify your portfolio to reduce risk and maximize opportunities.

Brand-able Domains: Consider acquiring brand-able domains that have potential value for start-ups, businesses, or specific industries. These domains should be easily recognizable and have potential for branding purposes.

Market Research: Conduct market research to understand the demand for specific types of virtual real estate and domain names. Identify potential buyers or target audiences for your digital assets.

Enhance Value: Develop or improve virtual real estate properties to increase their appeal and potential resale value. For domain names, consider adding content, creating landing pages, or improving search engine optimization (SEO).

Monetization Strategies: Explore monetization strategies for virtual real estate and domain names, such as leasing properties, selling domains through auctions, or brokering domain sales.

Sell or Lease: List your virtual real estate properties and domain names for sale or lease on relevant platforms and marketplaces. Use effective marketing strategies to attract potential buyers or lessees.

Stay Informed: Stay updated on industry trends, new developments in virtual real estate and domain flipping, and changes in the digital asset market. Adapt your strategies based on market developments.

By following these steps and consistently researching, acquiring, and marketing valuable digital assets, you can work towards making money through virtual real estate and domain flipping.

Chapter 14
Becoming an Influencer on Social Media:

An influencer in social media is an individual who has established credibility, authority, and a large following in a particular industry or niche. These individuals have the power to affect the purchasing decisions of others because of their expertise, knowledge, and relationship with their audience. Influencers are not just limited to celebrities or public figures; they can also be experts or enthusiasts in a specific area, such as fashion, beauty, fitness, travel, or technology. They use their platform to share their experiences, opinions, and recommendations with their followers and their influence can be seen in the way their audience engages with their content and the products or services they promote.

In today's digital age, social media influencers play a significant role in shaping consumer behaviour and trends. Their impact is felt across various platforms, including Instagram, YouTube, TikTok, and Twitter, where they have built a loyal and engaged following. Influencers are seen as trendsetters and tastemakers, and brands often collaborate with them to reach their target audience in a more authentic and relatable way. They have the ability to create viral content, spark conversations, and drive engagement, making them valuable partners for brands looking to increase their visibility and connect with potential customers.

One of the key characteristics of influencer in social media is their ability to create high-quality and engaging content that resonates with their audience. Whether it's through captivating visuals, informative videos, or compelling storytelling, influencers know how to capture the attention of their followers and keep them coming back for more. They understand the importance of authenticity and transparency in their interactions with their audience, which helps build trust and credibility. Their content often reflects their personal brand and values, allowing them to connect with their followers on a deeper level and establish a sense of community within their online platform.

In addition to creating compelling content, influencers also play a role in shaping conversations and driving social change. They have the power to raise awareness about important issues, advocate for causes they believe in, and mobilize their audience to take action. Whether it's promoting sustainability, diversity and inclusion, mental health awareness, or other social causes, influencers have the ability to use their platform for good and make a positive impact on society. Their influence extends beyond just promoting products or services; they have the potential to inspire and educate their audience on important matters that affect our world today.

Furthermore, influencers are adept at leveraging their social media presence to monetize their platform through various means. This can include brand partnerships, sponsored content, affiliate marketing, product collaborations, and even launching their own products or services. By partnering with brands that align with their values and resonate with their audience, influencers can create authentic and impactful marketing campaigns that drive results for both the brand and themselves. They have the ability to turn their passion into a profitable business while maintaining the trust and loyalty of their followers.

Another important aspect of being influencer in social media is the ability to adapt to the ever-changing landscape of digital marketing and social media trends. Influencers are constantly evolving and experimenting with new formats, platforms, and strategies to stay relevant and engage with their audience. They understand the importance of staying ahead of the curve and embracing innovation to continue growing their reach and impact. Whether it's embracing new features on social media platforms, exploring emerging trends, or collaborating with other influencers, they are always looking for ways to elevate their content and stay connected with their audience.

Influencer in social media is more than just someone with a large following; they are individuals who have built a strong personal brand, established trust with their audience, and have the power to shape opinions and behaviours. They are trendsetters, advocates, and entrepreneurs who leverage their influence to create meaningful connections with their followers and drive impact in the digital space. Their role extends beyond just promoting products; they have the ability to inspire change, drive conversations, and build communities around shared interests. As social media continues to play a central role in our lives, influencers will continue to be a driving force in shaping the way we consume content, make purchasing decisions, and engage with the world around us.

Becoming a known influencer on social media involves building a strong personal brand, engaging with your audience, and creating content that resonates with your followers. Here are the steps to consider when looking at how to make money online by becoming influencer on social media:

Choose Your Niche: Select a specific niche or area of expertise that aligns with your interests, skills, and the interests of your target audience. This could be fashion, beauty, fitness, travel, food, technology, or any other area of passion.

Define Your Brand: Develop a unique and authentic personal brand that reflects your personality, values, and expertise. Your brand should be consistent across all social media platforms you use.

Create High-Quality Content: Produce engaging and high-quality content that provides value to your audience. This can include photos, videos, blog posts, tutorials, reviews, and behind-the-scenes glimpses into your life or work.

Engage with Your Audience: Foster meaningful engagement with your audience by responding to comments, asking for feedback, and initiating conversations. Building a community around your content is essential for influencer growth.

Collaborate with Others: Collaborate with other influencers, brands, and content creators within your niche. This can help you reach new audiences and establish credibility within the industry.

Utilize Multiple Platforms: Use multiple social media platforms to expand your reach and engage with different audiences. This can include platforms such as Instagram, YouTube, TikTok, Twitter, Facebook, and LinkedIn.

Provide Value: Share content that educates, entertains, inspires, or solves problems for your audience. Providing value is key to building trust and loyalty with your followers.

Network and Build Relationships: Network with other influencers, industry professionals, and brands to expand your reach and create new opportunities for collaboration.

Stay Authentic: Be genuine and authentic in your interactions and content creation. Authenticity is a key factor in building trust with your audience.

Monetize Your Influence: Explore monetization opportunities such as sponsored content, brand partnerships, affiliate marketing, merchandise sales, and speaking engagements.

Analyze Your Performance: Use analytics tools provided by social media platforms to track the performance of your content and understand the demographics of your audience.

By following these steps and consistently creating valuable content, engaging with your audience, and building a strong personal brand, you can work towards becoming influencer on social media.

www.ingramcontent.com/pod-product-compliance
Lightning Source LLC
Chambersburg PA
CBHW071054240526
45471CB00015B/1881